EARLY YEARS
WORK-BASED
LEARNING

EARLY YEARS
WORK-BASED
LEARNING

LRC Stoke Park
GUILDFORD COLLEGE

Editor
Penny Farrelly

LearningMatters

First published in 2010 by Learning Matters Ltd

British Library Cataloguing in Publication Data
A CIP record for this book is available from the British Library.

ISBN: 978 1 84445 615 4

This book is also available in the following ebook formats:

Adobe ebook   ISBN: 978 1 84445 617 8
EPUB ebook   ISBN: 978 1 84445 616 1
Kindle   ISBN: 978 1 84445 949 0

Cover design by Topics
Text design by Bob Rowinski (Code 5)
Project management by Diana Chambers
Typeset by Kelly Winter
Printed by TJ International Ltd, Padstow, Cornwall

Learning Matters Ltd
33 Southernhay East
Exeter EX1 1NX
Tel: 01392 215560
info@learningmatters.co.uk
www.learningmatters.co.uk

FSC
Mixed Sources
Product group from well-managed
forests and other controlled sources
Cert no. SGS-COC-2482
www.fsc.org
© 1996 Forest Stewardship Council

Contents

Editor and contributors

Penny Farrelly
Penny comes from a Health Visiting background and is passionate about the health and well-being of young children. She teaches evidence-based practice on the Specialist Community Public Health Nursing programme and has helped to develop the Sector Endorsed Foundation Degree Early Years and the BA (Hons) Practice Development (Early Years), for both of which she is a Senior Lecturer. She is also co-course leader for the Foundation Degree Working with Children and Young People, all at Buckinghamshire New University.

Patricia Johnson
Tricia is a Senior Lecturer on the Sector Endorsed Foundation Degree Early Years and the BA (Hons) Practice Development (Early Years) at Buckinghamshire New University, both of which she helped to develop. She is an experienced Early Years practitioner, she helped at her local preschool and then combined her nursing qualification with a lifelong ambition to work with children, she was employed by the Norland College for fourteen years where she worked in and then managed two of the childcare areas caring for children aged from ten days to nine years. Tricia was a member of the local EYDCP, chaired the Quality and Training sub group and was involved in writing the Guidance to accompany the National Standards for the Regulation of Day Care with the DfES.

Carol Rogers
Carol is an experienced Early Years practitioner having worked as a childminder in preschools and currently as deputy manager for a respite play centre for children with additional needs. She has also had significant experience of teaching and learning as head of curriculum in a further education college. This role included teaching on a wide range of Early Years' courses and new course development including a Foundation Degree for Early Years. Carol is currently senior lecturer and course leader for the Early Years Foundation Degree at Buckinghamshire New University.

Jane Wright
Jane teaches on a range of programmes related to children and young people, including Foundation, BSc and MSc levels. She worked for six years as a community school nurse in

Buckinghamshire. She is the co-course leader for the Foundation Degree Working with Children and Young People at Buckinghamshire New University. Jane also teaches child development studies on the FD in Early Years.

1 INTRODUCTION: WORK-BASED LEARNING FOR EARLY YEARS AND EARLY CHILDHOOD STUDIES

CHAPTER OBJECTIVES

By the end of this chapter you will:

- know what is meant by a Foundation Degree;
- understand the term work-based learning;
- understand the importance of the work-based learning approach in children's settings;
- appreciate the links to EYFS standards made by the Foundation Degree in Early Years.

Introduction

The government is committed to improving the educational level of the children's workforce and to having an Early Years Professional (EYP) with a degree in each childcare setting by 2010 (DfES, 2006). There are, therefore, a growing number of people finding themselves studying for a Foundation Degree who previously had no intention of ever doing so.

The aim of this book is to encourage and support students studying for a Foundation Degree in Early Years, Early Childhood Studies or Working with Children and Young People. One observation of the team teaching Early Years at Buckinghamshire New University is that the students who study these courses are amazed to find themselves in college studying for a degree. They have often achieved few qualifications and have had negative experiences of the education system in the past. Consequently, they lack confidence in their abilities and need a lot of support and reassurance from lecturing staff when they start their studies. Hopefully, your experience of studying for a Foundation Degree will encourage you to start thinking of learning as a lifelong process and one that can bring you many rewards in addition to your award. These may include:

- the long-term friendships you may develop with other students;
- the support of other like-minded professionals;
- a love of learning;

- sharing experience with others;
- confidence that your qualification, knowledge and experience puts you on an equal footing with other professionals.

This book aims to address your concerns and alleviate your anxieties as you commence studying by talking you through aspects of work-based study and by offering simple activities to do that will help you to get organised and ensure you feel more confident about the undertaking. Case studies and comments from current students will be offered to 'bring the text to life' and to reassure you that you are not alone in your fears. Foundation Degrees are quite a new thing and students are often confused about what the term means, so the introduction will start by clarifying their role and purpose while explaining work-based learning and why it suits the Early Years sector.

The introduction will also present example profiles of Early Years Foundation Degree and Early Years Professional Status (EYS) candidates, exploring the skills and knowledge needed. An overview of the content of the course in terms of skills, knowledge and practitioner elements will also be offered. Chapter 2 then moves on to present a brief history of Early Years provision in the UK exploring current provision, policy and legislation and the importance of professionalising the workforce – the move to a graduate profession.

Chapter 3 explores the importance of recognising your own learning needs and the importance of developing a balance between study and work, before discussing research skills and methods which may be used in Early Years settings and the particular issues involved when dealing with children. Students are offered ways of presenting critical evaluation, report writing and presentations. The role of the mentor in Early Years settings and receiving feedback is discussed, before moving on to the subject of developing a portfolio.

Chapter 4 explores what it means to be an EYP and how to get the most out of work experiences by sharing these in classroom debates and discussions. Reflection is a key activity in vocational courses and for these students it is the foundation for the whole undertaking. This chapter explains why it is important, how it links to work-based learning, what it means and how to do it effectively.

This leads on to Chapter 5 which discusses issues around supporting children's learning and development in practice while developing your specialist knowledge, giving a brief overview of the theories of how children learn, looking at individual learning styles and how Early Years professionals can best facilitate children's learning by providing an effective learning environment in their setting.

Chapter 6 presents some current debates in Early Years education and provision, and explains to the reader how specific knowledge of certain issues can help them with their wider knowledge and skills. It explores international perspectives in Early Years education and discusses staff gender issues in the Early Years. The issue of inclusive Early Years provision is debated before looking at the changing position of the child in the centre of this field as the rights of the child are explored.

Finally, the future of Early Years and the Professional Status is discussed. Chapter 7 looks forward to the role of the EYP in the future, imagining a sector where professionals work in partnership with others, often in centres where children and family services are brought together on one site, led by staff who have completed their degrees and have continued their professional development, thus allowing them to take a leadership role of multi-professional teams. It stresses the importance of continuing professional development and identifies some issues likely to have an influence on Early Years settings in the future.

Foundation Degrees: what are they and where have they come from?

The Foundation Degree (FD) is still a relatively new idea on the education scene. It was introduced by the Department for Education and Skills (DfES) in 2000 as a way of providing the graduates needed to address the higher technical and associate professional level skills shortages within the labour market.

Since that time, key agencies and organisations in the education and training infrastructure have been actively involved in implementing the policy on a nationwide basis.

The award straddles the further education/higher education (FE/HE) worlds with delivery in either setting but validated and monitored by HE institutions. It also includes employer involvement in both the development and delivery phases.

The FD is different from anything that has gone before in the sense that it allows you to 'earn while you learn'. It provides you with an opportunity to gain a degree while using your own work experiences to inform your assignments and course work. Your experience is clearly valued and you are expected to explore and share your experiences in the classroom, so learners all help each other and gain from each other's experience.

The need for flexible, multi-skilled staff provides a strong case for the FD, which can make an important contribution to meeting this need by providing broad-based knowledge, transferable skills, including lifelong learning, and the capacity to adapt to changing job roles.

ACTIVITY
Can you think of any ways in which professionalising the work force in children's settings will benefit the children there?

What is a Foundation Degree?

FDs were primarily introduced to address specific labour market shortages at the associate professional level. FDs also provide an ideal development opportunity for those within the workforce, as well as a route to higher education for those with vocational qualifications.

The FD rates the same academically as the first two years of a three-year Honours degree at a UK university. It can be achieved in two years by part-time study because it is work-based and in an applied discipline. Currently, about 50,000 students (mostly adult and part-time) are following

FDs in England. Subjects range from Nuclear Decommissioning to Community Development and Early Years! Almost all FDs offer progression to an Honours degree.

The key features of an FD are that you will be able to:

- develop your specialist technical knowledge and skills of Early Years practice;
- structure your learning around your employment;
- develop your motivation and qualifications, and therefore benefit from increased career opportunities;
- continue to earn while learning – there is no need to give up your job to do an FD;
- receive teaching and support from academics, practitioners and employers, and share experiences with a wide range of other practitioners.

How is the FD delivered?

- Flexible and diverse study methods, including work-based learning (WBL), lectures, seminars, tutorials, distance learning and on-line support.
- Students study in the workplace and should have an allocated mentor to support their learning in practice.

WBL is integral to FDs – many students will study while working full- or part-time. Some students will receive financial assistance from employers, while others may receive time off or other support such as workplace mentoring.

What is work-based learning?

The key principle behind WBL is a wish to recognise higher learning wherever it has taken place and reward those who have achieved it with university qualifications (Durrant et al., 2008). WBL is not so much about being taught by someone but about being an independent learner'; this involves developing a higher level of understanding of your own practice, and managing and taking responsibility for your own work and learning priorities. This may involve sitting down with your personal tutor and discussing what your own areas of strengths and weaknesses are so that you can jointly develop an individualised learning contract, which clearly details what the learner will do to meet identified learning needs and achieve specific learning outcomes.

WBL is increasingly being used as a mode of study for employed people and as a way of introducing positive changes in practice within the workplace. It focuses on learning in, and from the workplace where you work, rather than a set curriculum providing the focus for the learning programme. It promotes awareness of the workplace as a learning environment and uses this to extend the learner's capability and individual effectiveness. Although the university will offer you a structured curriculum in terms of modules of study area, you will be doing most of your learning at your place of work, and then sharing your experiences with other professionals in the university or college, so you will be using your workplace as your focus for study. The main feature of WBL is for you to demonstrate your ability to reflect on your skills, knowledge and approach to your work (Durrant et al., 2008).

WBL programmes are designed to promote professional and personal development, and are intended to benefit both learners and the workplace. Interpersonal, interprofessional, intellectual and practical skills are developed through each learner's recognition and reflection upon his or her professional development, and the application of this to the workplace (Rawlings, 2008).

What types of learners have undertaken Foundation Degrees in Early Years or Childhood Studies?

Example profiles of Early Years Foundation Degree and EYPS candidates

Childminder Lynn is studying for a Foundation Degree in Early Years. Like many learners she has found it difficult to balance her work, family and study commitments, particularly with her working patterns. She has valued the support of other students and her tutors while studying. As her studies are mainly based in her place of work, she feels she has not had to segregate work and study. She attends the university for one day a week and has particularly enjoyed the opportunity to share experiences with other students who are working in childcare settings, though she is unique in working with more autonomy and in more isolation in her role than they are.

Classroom assistant Katrina is studying for a Foundation Degree in Childhood Studies and works in a secondary school with the Special Educational Needs (SEN) team. She has two young children herself and has had very little opportunity to pursue her own career. She sees this course as a stepping stone to wider opportunities, and knows she wants to continue to work with children. The course suits her well as the school allows her to attend college for one day a week and she feels she really benefits from the support she gets from the other students on the course. She has learnt a lot about how to problem solve in certain situations she encounters regularly in her workplace from others on the course with more experience in her field. Katrina says she has missed coming in to college to meet up with the other students when there have been holidays and really feels she is developing a 'taste for learning'.

Early Years day nursery worker Cathy had a number of different careers before moving into childcare when her own children started school. She began by helping out for a few hours a week and is now the deputy manager of a large and busy nursery, a role that involves staff management and training, planning and dealing with parents, as well as caring for the children. When the government announced its plans to ensure that every nursery setting had someone in place with degree level qualifications she put herself forward to study for the Foundation Degree in Early Years. She has found the most difficult aspect is juggling the demands of a family, work and study, and sometimes feels that she is carrying out none of those roles as effectively as she should be, but her family is very supportive and she wants to act as a role model for her daughters who see her studying and realise that it is not something you just do at school.

Family support worker Jan is working for the local council as a family support worker, which involves her going out to support families who have been identified, whether by the health visitor or by the child's school, as having problems, usually coping with behaviour or with facilitating development. Jan's own children are all away at university or in their first jobs and she felt this was the time to start some studying. This was a bit daunting as she had not written academically since leaving school 30 years previously. However, having been into the university to meet the staff she felt that with the support being offered and by being able to use her wide range of experience she was prepared to 'give it a go' and study for a Foundation Degree in Childhood Studies to give some underpinning knowledge to the work she does. Since starting the course she has found a wealth of contacts and support through the other students in her group and says she wishes she had done it years ago!

ACTIVITY

Would your family support you in the type of endeavour illustrated above? What about your employer, what support would they be willing to offer?

Early Years Professional Status

There has always been a wide range of settings for under-fives in the UK; this currently includes local authority day nurseries and family centres, playgroups, private and workplace nurseries, childminders and Children's Centres. There are also local (education) authority and private nursery classes and schools, as well as a very large number of four-year-olds in infant school classes. All these different groups have different aims and goals; they have a range of admissions criteria and hours of opening, and they are staffed by people – largely women – with different training, different levels of pay and different conditions of service. There is also a class differential in their use, with the children using local authority provision tending to be from the lower socio-economic class, while middle-class children are more likely to have access to private provision.

Even within the state sector there have been important differences between the services provided. Day nurseries often provide whole daycare and are administered and staffed by those with two years' training and with the primary emphasis being on young children's social and emotional development. These day nurseries do not normally employ teachers. Maintained sector nursery classes and schools, by contrast, are administered and staffed by nursery officers with two years' training or a teaching assistant. The primary emphasis here is on young children learning through a quality curriculum. There is, therefore, a real need to ensure that there is some standardisation in terms of what is offered and in terms of the qualifications staff in these settings have in order to ensure the best possible care for the children. One factor that impacted on this was the government White Paper *Every Child Matters* (DfES, 2003) and the subsequent 2004 Children Act had far-reaching implications for all those working in the childcare sector.

The focus changed from being on the services to being on children and their families, and was focused on tackling poverty and on improving outcomes for children and young people, reducing the gaps between those who do well and those who do not. Young children and their families do not see their needs for healthcare, education, jobs or housing as separate entities, and neither should the professionals working with them.

Many of the recent developments in Early Years provision pre-dated the *Every Child Matters* (ECM) agenda and were influential in its development. Sure Start local programmes, for example, which evolved out of the New Labour government's cross-department review of services for children under eight in 1998 were established to provide support for families in the early months and years of a child's life, with a strong emphasis on prevention. They were also required to be set up in, and by, local communities, and to both employ and have on their management committee, representatives of health, education, social services, the voluntary sector and parents. At around the same time, the 'early excellence centres' initiative was launched, building on the earlier combined nursery centres with a focus on integrated education and care for young children, providing support for families, child and family health services, and for other services such as childminder networks.

Every Child Matters and the 2004 Children Act were, therefore, building on good Early Years practice in their response to the failures in the system that were identified in Lord Laming's report on the death of Victoria Climbié. Five key themes were identified.

- Building strong foundations in the Early Years.
- A stronger focus on parenting and families.
- Earlier interventions and effective protection.
- Better accountability and integration locally, regionally and nationally.
- Reform of the workforce.

The overall aims can be summarised as improving outcomes for all children and narrowing the gap between those who do well and those who do not; improving and integrating universal services; more specialist help to promote opportunity and prevent problems; reconfiguring services around the child and family; and sharing responsibility for safeguarding children.

All this reflects a growing concern to move away from a time when, historically, childcare was only discussed as a need of working parents. The needs of the children have often been pushed into the background but, more recently, there has been a willingness to think of care and education as a combined effort for the benefit of the child, independent of the employment status of the parents (Willan et al., 2010). Keeping the needs of children in mind may also improve the quality of childcare provision throughout the country.

To this end, the government has developed several initiatives to encourage and support professionals in developing shared knowledge and a shared language of child development and teaching. In 2006, the Early Years Professional Standards were produced (CWDC, 2006), setting out training routes that aim to develop a world-class workforce to improve outcomes for children.

The government aims to have an EYP in every full daycare setting by 2015 and in every children's centre by 2010. According to the Children's Workforce Development Council (CWDC) website, an EYP will:

- take responsibility for leading and managing play, care and learning;
- develop, introduce, lead and supervise development work;
- act as a team leader and inspire others;
- possess up-to-date knowledge and understanding of Early Years practices;
- help colleagues to develop and improve their practice.

> **ACTIVITY**
> What are the advantages for children and their families of being cared for by a professional workforce?

Standards for EYPS are grouped together under the following headings.

- Knowledge and understanding.
- Effective practice.
- Relationships with children.
- Communication and working together with families and carers.

All candidates for EYPS have to demonstrate through their practice that they have attained the required level of competence, and it is anticipated that in the future only those with EYPS will lead the delivery of the Early Years Foundation Stage (EYFS) (Miller and Cable, 2008).

The EYP is intended to be a change agent who will raise standards in Early Years settings, in particular to lead practice in the EYFS and support and mentor other practitioners. They are required to be graduates and to demonstrate they can meet the above set of national standards. This is achieved by a choice of four pathways which are centrally funded by CWDC (CWDC, 2006).

CHAPTER SUMMARY

- This chapter has introduced you to the idea of Foundation Degrees and explored the impetus for, and the advantages of, utilising work-based learning.
- The range of childcare settings has been outlined and the suggestion that the government wants to see a graduate in each daycare setting by 2015 has been presented.
- Some typical Foundation Degree students have been profiled for you to give you an idea of the type of person who has found studying in this way particularly useful.
- The role of the EYP has been outlined.

REFERENCES
Children's Workforce Development Council (CWDC) (2006) *Early Years Professional Prospectus.* Leeds: CWDC.
DfES (Department for Education and Skills) (2003) *Every Child Matters*. London: Stationery Office.
Durrant, A, Rhodes, G, Young, D (2009) *Getting Started with University Level Work-based Learning.* London: Middlesex University Press.
HM Government (2004) *The Children Act*. London: Stationery Office.

Miller, L and Cable, C (2008) *Professionalism in the Early Years*. London: Hodder Education.

Rawlings, A (2008) *Studying Early Years: A Guide to Work-Based Learning*. Maidenhead: Open University Press.

Willan, J, Parker-Rees, J and Savage, J (2010) *Early Childhood Studies*. 3rd edition. Exeter: Learning Matters.

FURTHER READING

Children's Workforce Development Council http//cwdcouncil.org.uk.

Department for Education and Skills (DfES) (2003) *Every Child Matters*. London: Stationery Office.

Miller, L and Cable, C (2008) *Professionalism in the Early Years*. London: Hodder Education.

Rawlings, A (2008) *Studying Early Years: A Guide to Work-Based Learning*. Maidenhead: Open University Press.

2 THE EARLY YEARS SECTOR IN THE UK: THE CURRENT CONTEXT

Children become the victims or the beneficiaries of adult actions.

(Cunningham, 2006, cited in Laming, 2009, p2)

CHAPTER OBJECTIVES

By the end of this chapter you will:

- gain an understanding of historical and current perspectives of childcare and education in the UK;
- be able to evaluate current provision, policies and legislation;
- understand the changes to the Early Years workforce, moving towards a graduate workforce.

Introduction

This chapter will discuss childcare provision and education in the UK and will make comparisons between historic and current provision, legislation and include the influence of political and economic factors.

As we begin to discuss childcare provision and education, it is important to consider the context of the child within this. Is the well-being of children at the heart of all that drives and governs change or is the social and economic need of the country the stronger determinant?

When comparing current and historic Early Years practice, it could be said that we have come full circle, that history repeats itself, and so by examining the history of policies and practices relating to children current policy and practice can be better understood. It is also important to consider how children are regarded by considering and defining childhood both historically and currently, and how this impacts on childcare provision and education. The government's National Childcare Strategy, *Meeting the Childcare Challenge*, places high value on children, families and education. There has been unprecedented investment in children's services with considerable and rapid change in the Early Years workforce.

The aims of the National Childcare strategy are that *Every child deserves the best possible start in life*, but it also suggests that sufficient quality childcare provision *is good for children, parents, communities and the national economy.* The strategy also goes on to assert that

> *Suitable childcare is a great benefit to parents so they can balance their working lives and domestic commitments and is a vital route out of poverty for families enabling parents to work, pursue a career, learn or train, confident that their children are being cared for in a safe and stimulating environment*

(DfEE, 1998, p3)

While it could be argued that, as future generations, children have an important impact on society, we also need to consider the impact that society, legislation and policy have on children and their childhoods. Lowe, cited in Maynard and Thomas (2009), poses the question, *to what extent is childhood a social construct or is it a stage of life all human beings go through?* Childhood is a life stage. However, it is also socially constructed and will differ across and between societies and cultures depending on the economic need for children to contribute to the family. In Western cultures childhood is a life stage where the child is viewed as vulnerable, to be nurtured, protected and developed through education to achieve their full potential.

History provides some interesting and contrasting views of childhood care and education. Early accounts of childhood education are of gender and class-biased education, with little or no care or consideration for the development of the whole child. Despite this, some early pioneers recognised that children needed to have care as well as education. Philosophers as early as Plato proposed that educators should consider the development of children's well-being as well as educational attainment. He recognised the importance of play as a learning tool and yet it is only being given value again today within the context of the EYFS. There are a number of other significant individuals, including Froebel, Isaacs and McMillan, who also recognised the value of play and the importance of good health and well-being as crucial to children's learning and development. Health, well-being and play are all acknowledged as fundamental to and embedded in *Every Child Matters* and the EYFS, the current government initiatives and policies driving Early Years care and education.

Childhood in medieval society and the Middle Ages

Whereas current Early Years policy is influenced by government, historically, early education was provided by the Church, promoting views of strict discipline and harsh treatment of children. The *spare the rod spoil the child* (Cunningham, 2006, p29) view was the dominant practice as a necessary and acceptable way to rid children of evil characteristics to enable them to become effective adults. While this was the majority view, there were some, including the thirteenth-century Archbishop of Canterbury, St Anselm, who is said to have stated *a child is like a plant, it needs care and attention* (Cunningham, 2006, p29), who recognised the vulnerability and importance of supporting and caring for the holistic development of children.

Historian Philippe Aries suggests that the idea of childhood did not begin to exist until the seventeenth century.

In medieval society the idea of childhood did not exist; this is not to suggest that children were neglected, forsaken or despised. The idea of childhood is not to be confused with affection for children: it corresponds to an awareness of the particular nature which distinguishes the child from the adult. In medieval society this awareness did not exist.

(Aries, 1962, cited in Schaffer, 2008, p21)

Some evidence of this view is emphasised in medieval art; early paintings of children often portray them as mini adults, with adult facial features.

During this period, the focus of education changed from adults to children. This resulted in a change in status for children from being little adults to children *not being ready for life* (Aries, 1962, p412) and needing to be treated differently. Furthermore, this led to formal educational instruction for the more affluent families, but, for poorer children, education was based on learning life skills rather than school-based learning. These life skills were learnt by observing and modelling behaviours and experiences of parents, learning the skills they would need as adults.

The medieval period governed by the Church proposed that children were born evil and were in need of improvement and their souls saving. The Church placed the responsibility for the saving of children on their parents, which also made the parents responsible for social learning. The focus of family life also changed, having a greater moral and spiritual function, and with this the status of children within the family altered, valuing all children equally rather than favouring the eldest child.

As school and education provision developed, there became a strong focus on care as well as education. During the seventeenth century there was a strong ethos of care linked to religious expectations that parents would provide for the development and education of social skills.

Historically, parents were measured by the Church, which was the dominant authority of the time, as opposed to society, the media and government in more modern times. Some historic views would suggest a lack of parental care and concern regarding children, but evidence of the growth of legislation, education and care provision would perhaps dispute this view. Cunningham proposes that this period of time mirrors the twenty-first century with regard to parental anxiety in relation to the expectations of society on parenting skills, suggesting *Parental care set alongside parental neglect and cruelty* (2006, p21). In the Middle Ages parents were judged by the Church, today by the government. Dunn and Layard suggest that the *greatest responsibility is on parents . . . a key resource for every child and future adult* (2009, p155). Parents were a key resource for children in history as role models and teachers of life skills. Today, much of children's learning now takes place outside the home in daycare and education settings, but parents are still valued as the child's first and most enduring educator. This view is reinforced throughout present legislation with parental responsibility established within the Children Act 1989 and the Ten Year Childcare Strategy, *Choice for Parents, the Best Start for Children*.

Parents will always have the primary responsibility for the care and well-being of their children. It is up to parents to decide what sort of childcare they want for their children. This is not a matter for the Government. But it is the Government's responsibility to ensure that parents have access to services to enable them to make genuine choices.

(DfEE, 1998, p6)

Both historic and current policy and practice recognise the value and influence that parents have on children's lives, but how significant is government policy on influencing parents in the changing shape of childhood? Aries (1962) advocated three factors influencing the changing perception of childhood during the Middle Ages. First, children were being viewed as vulnerable, valuable and in need of protection; second, there was a need for discipline and training; and third, schools and education were developing. These factors predisposed the changes in family attitudes to children.

So, the profile of childhood developed from the medieval view of children as adults in waiting, needing to be delivered from evil through education and as the property of their parents, to the child being viewed as a labourer and economic prospect and then as a school child, to the present view of childhood as a distinct life stage where children are nurtured and valued as individuals. However, this change for children, particularly within the workforce, may have come from changes in the economy rather than the well-being of the child.

ACTIVITY

Consider how childhood is defined today. Is it an adult concept that children have to live within?

If childhood is an adult construct, what influences and shapes it – politics, society, culture?

The Industrial Revolution to 1944

The Industrial Revolution had a significant impact in shaping and changing the development of care and education provision for children. Legislation to protect children from exploitation by restricting the number of hours worked, alongside the mechanisation of factories, led to a reduction in the need for child labour. This resulted in children becoming a social problem as they roamed the streets while their parents worked. Consequently, the introduction of compulsory schooling and protective legislation influenced the decline in child labour. There was also social change for childhood: the reduction in child labour for working-class children enabled them to become children – having a childhood and going to school. This signalled the beginnings of care provision for children with the recognition that they needed both care and education. It was during this period that wealthy merchants, such as Thomas Coram, set up the Foundling Hospital and Dr Thomas Barnardo opened his first orphanage, indicating the beginnings of formal care outside of the family for children in need.

In 1905, school inspector Katherine Bathurst's report for the Education Board highlighted the unsuitability of schoolrooms for children under five. The report argued that schoolrooms were poorly ventilated, overcrowded and unhygienic, and the desks were too high for small children. Bathurst believed that harsh discipline and a strict curriculum were unsuitable for 3–5-year-olds and proposed separate facilities for children under five in the form of a kindergarten system. In reality, however, this did not begin to happen until after the Second World War. During and following this war the role of women changed, as did the structure of the population, resulting in a smaller workforce. It became necessary for women to be economically active. The Ministry of Education set up state nurseries, although these were perhaps motivated by economic need rather than consideration for the care and well-being of children.

The movement towards better care and conditions for young children in the early twentieth century continued with the campaign of sisters Rachel and Margaret McMillan for school meals for children. The sisters believed that hungry children could not learn and convinced the government to pass the Provision of School Meals Act in 1906. The legislation accepted the argument put forward by the McMillan sisters that if the state insisted on compulsory education it must take responsibility for the proper nourishment of schoolchildren. This was followed by the inclusion of medical clinics in schools. In 1914, the sisters started an Open-Air Nursery School & Training Centre in Peckham, promoting the importance of health well-being as crucial to ensuring successful learning and development. The need to consider the holistic development and the individuality of the child was further promoted by Susan Isaacs, an educational psychologist and psychoanalyst who, as head of the Malting House School between 1924 and 1927, claimed that children learned best through their own play. Isaacs also advocated the importance of promoting independence and individualised learning programmes, especially for young children. So there began an increasing lobby for specific and different provision for children under five.

Despite the efforts of practitioners and pioneers such as the McMillan sisters and Susan Isaacs, the government did not acknowledge the value of education for children under five until the 1944 Education Act. This Act stated that local authorities should provide nursery education. However, this did not happen as resources were focused on mainstream school provision. Although there were no challenges to this failure to meet the requirements to provide Early Years provision, there continued to be a series of reports highlighting the value of nursery education. The reality of the 1944 Education Act was that due to limited funding, nurseries did not flourish as statutory provision.

1945 to the present day

Following the Second World War, childcare provision developed slowly and, in 1948 when first regulations for nurseries and childminders were introduced, this came from *moral panic about the dangers of accidental harm to children when in the care of people other than their mothers* (Baldock et al., 2009, p15). These regulations focused on the prevention of accidents and infection. The main emphasis of legislation was based on maintaining the physical care of children.

Childcare provision began to increase in the 1960s with the start of the preschool playgroup movement, the aim of which was to provide community-based part-time provision for children.

The Plowden Report in 1967 provided a line of reasoning both for and against the growth of nursery education. The argument for stated that the benefits of nursery education improved children's social skills, health and welfare, as well as providing educational opportunities. The arguments against suggested that children were best off at home with their mothers who were able to provide the same experiences as those of nurseries. Nevertheless, the final recommendations of the report stated:

There should be a large expansion of nursery, a measure of adult support as in the good home . . . education and a start should be made as soon as possible.

(Plowden, 1967, p132)

Despite the recommendations of the report, the expansion of nursery provision did not happen. Similarly, the 1972 White Paper, *Framework for Expansion*, proposed that nursery education would be provided for all children who wanted it by 1980. This led to some government support for Early Years provision. In spite of this, the economic recession of that period prevented the full implementation of additional nursery places.

The change of government in 1997 initiated the rapid and significant development of the Early Years sector, starting with the introduction of the National Childcare Strategy, *Meeting the Childcare Challenge*, an ambitious strategy of which the most noteworthy element has been tackling poverty. The government saw childcare services and provision as fundamental to combating poverty, to improving opportunities for children and to engaging parents back into the workforce. Early Years policy became a priority in meeting this aim by providing *good quality, affordable childcare for children aged 0 to 14 in every neighbourhood* (DfEE, 1998, p7).

When the National Childcare Strategy was introduced in 1998, there was a national shortage of childcare places and one of the key aims of the strategy was to provide good quality and affordable childcare provision. The strategy recognised that:

For too long, the UK has lagged behind in developing good quality, affordable and accessible childcare. The approach taken by previous governments to the formal childcare sector has been to leave it almost exclusively to the market. But this simply hasn't worked. And the voluntary sector has been expected to provide, with little Government support, most of the services for children.

(DfES, 1998, p5)

As well as recognising a shortage of childcare places, there was acknowledgement that the quality of available provision was variable, and to improve the consistency and quality of provision stronger partnership working between local authority departments was established. This led to the development of Early Years Development and Childcare Partnerships, which have evolved into the current children's services. Partnership working with parents also became a priority.

A significant investment in funding enabled the expansion of childcare with neighbourhood nurseries and out-of-school initiatives promoted by the government, but there was also growth within the private and voluntary sectors, including significant expansion of private daycare facilities. In 2005, Sure Start Children's Centres were established to deliver government intentions of supporting families and reducing poverty. The centres were set up within local authority areas of deprivation, bringing together a range of services including childcare, early education, health and social services, as well as voluntary, private and community organisations and parents themselves, to provide integrated services for young children. These have evolved into current Children's Centres, with a target for a children's centre in every community by 2015.

The momentum for change escalated further in 2003 following the recommendations of the Laming Report into the death of Victoria Climbié. The outcome was the publication of a Green

Paper *Every Child Matters* (DfES, 2003), which brought about further development and unprecedented change to Early Years services and underpins all current legislation and practice relating to working with children. The Children Act 2004 provides the legislative spine for the delivery of the ECM agenda. This was strengthened further with the Childcare Act of 2006, the first legislation specifically for Early Years, instigated to implement the Early Years Foundation Stage (EYFS) Framework and to place specific duties on local authorities to ensure the provision of sufficient childcare places and improving quality. The Early Years Foundation Stage is the framework developed to deliver the ECM outcomes, bringing together the Curriculum Guidance for the Foundation Stage, Birth to Three Matters and the National Standards for under 8s Day care and Childminding, combining both care and education.

The impetus continued with the publication of the Children's Plan in 2007, which was introduced to ensure that the government's policy promoting the development and delivery of improvements to children and families remained prominent. It identifies progress made within the past ten years and sets the agenda for continuing development for the next ten years. The aim and principles of the Children's Plan are:

> *To make England the best place in the world for children and young people.*
>
> (DCSF, 2007, p2)

> - *Government does not bring up children – parents do – so government needs to do more to back parents and families.*
> - *All children have the potential to succeed and should go as far as their talents can take them.*
> - *Children and young people need to enjoy their childhood as well as grow up prepared for adult life.*
> - *Services need to be shaped by and responsive to children, young people and families, not designed around professional boundaries.*
> - *It is always better to prevent failure than tackle a crisis later.*
>
> (DCSF, 2007, p4)

The Children's Plan also states:

> *The single most important factor in delivering our aspirations for children is a world class workforce able to provide highly personalised support, so we will continue to drive up quality and capacity of those working in the children's workforce.*
>
> (DCSF, 2007, p11)

Parallel to the expansion in childcare provision has been the growth and professionalism of the workforce. The concept of the Early Years professional is relatively new. Historically, teaching was a male-dominated profession whose role was to educate. How times have changed, with current roles within Early Years being female-dominated and encompassing both care and education within the role. We have moved from a perception of baby farmers, as early childminders were regarded in the 1950s, to the 'mum's army', which was attributed to the preschool movement of the 1960s where the workforce was predominantly parents and unqualified, through to today and the current requirement of a highly skilled and qualified graduate workforce outlined by present legislation and policy. The statutory welfare requirements of the Early Years Foundation Stage also places a requirement on providers to employ *suitable* persons (DfES, 2007, p19), ensuring that those working with children have *appropriate qualifications training, skills and knowledge* (DfES, 2007, p20), thus recognising for the first time the significant importance of the role played by the Early Years workforce in supporting the care, learning and development of children.

The Children's Workforce Development Council (CWDC) was established in 2005 to support the implementation of *Every Child Matters*, and to oversee the quality and delivery of the EYPS. EYPS are the government's vision for achieving a graduate-led workforce by having an EYP in every daycare setting by 2015. The aim of the EYP is to improve the quality of practice in Early Years settings by leading and supporting other practitioners to become skilled and knowledgeable reflective practitioners. The philosophy behind this is to establish a highly skilled and qualified workforce that in turn will provide high-quality provision for the children in their care, thus meeting government aims of enabling children to have the best possible start in life.

In December 2008, the government introduced the 2020 Children and Young People's Workforce Strategy, further promoting their vision for workforce development. It identifies four key principles that the Early Years workforce should strive towards.

- **Ambitious** for every child and young person.
- **Excellent** in their practice.
- **Committed** to partnership and integrated working.
- **Respected** and valued as professionals.

So, to date, the most significant changes to childcare and education provision resulting from recent government initiatives include:

- an increase in provision;
- the development of a qualification framework;
- the introduction of the EYFS;
- a graduate-led workforce.

ACTIVITY

Identify changes in the roles and responsibilities of Early Years practitioners today and in the past.

Consider your role within your work setting. How has this changed in the last ten years?

Timeline of Childcare and Education Provision

- **Around 350BC Plato** believed that educators should be considering the development of children's well-being as well as educational attainment.
- **1592–1670 Joan-Amos Comenius** recognised the value of family to the education of children.
- **1632–1704 John Locke** advocated learning through play.
- **1712–1778 Jean Jacques Rousseau** also advocated learning through play, emphasising the importance of experimentation and flexibility in education and development.

- **1816 Robert Owen**, a Scottish Mill owner, set up schools for the children of his workers with a focus on care and activity. Owen is recognised as setting up the first nursery school in this country.
- **1833 Factory Act** – passed by the government and intended to improve conditions for children working in factories. It introduced a compulsory two hours' schooling each day for children. This was the first time that children of all backgrounds in the UK had access to education.
- **1870 Thomas Barnardo** established a school and orphanage to care for children orphaned by an outbreak of cholera in east London. Following societal changes in the mid-20th century, Barnardos changed its focus from the direct care of children to fostering and adoption. The last traditional orphanage closed in 1989 and the charity now focuses on work with some robust campaigning on Sarah's Law, asylum-seeking children, children in care, young carers and, most prominently, child poverty.
- **1870 Elementary Education Act** – drafted by William Forster developed school districts and school boards.
- **1880 Education Act** – made school attendance compulsory for all children up to the age of ten.
- **1884 The London Society for the Prevention of Cruelty to Children** was founded. Its aim then was to protect children from cruelty, support vulnerable families, campaign for changes to the law and raise awareness about abuse. It changed its name to The National Society for the Prevention of Cruelty to Children (NSPCC) in 1889. Its aim to end child cruelty remains the same.
- **1902 Margaret McMillan** successfully campaigned for the establishment of school medical inspections.
- **1905 Bathurst Report** – Katherine Bathurst argued that harsh discipline and a strict curriculum were unsuitable for 3–5-year-olds and proposed a kindergarten system.
- **1906 Provision of School Meals Act** – Margaret and Rachel McMillan, following a campaign, introduced free school meals under the 1906 Provision of School Meals Act. Opened first clinic dedicated to schoolchildren in 1906.
- **1914 Rachel and Margaret McMillan** – Open-Air Nursery School established.
- **1924 Susan Isaacs** – founded the Malting House School, with a curriculum designed to further the *individual* development of children.
- **1926 The Hadow Report** – During the 1920s and 1930s Sir Henry Hadow (1859–1937) chaired a consultative committee that was responsible for several important reports on education in England. In 1926, a report entitled *The Education of the Adolescent* looked at primary education in detail for the first time. It prioritised activity and experience, rather than rote learning, and discussed, for the first time, the specific needs of children with learning difficulties. The report also made the important recommendation of limiting class sizes to a maximum of thirty children. In 1931, another report was published: *The Primary School* was influenced by the educational ideas of Swiss psychologist Jean Piaget and advocated a style of teaching based on children's interests.
- **1944 Education Act** – Saw the introduction of the tripartite system. The Act introduced three different types of school: Grammar schools for the more academic pupil; Secondary Modern schools for a more practical, non-academic style of education; and Technical schools for specialist practical education. Pupils were allocated to a

particular type of school by taking an examination called the 11-Plus, which was also introduced under the Act. Secondary education now became free for all and the school-leaving age rose to 15.

- **1948 Nursery and Childminder Regulation Act set up.** Local authority children's departments set up under 1948 Children Act, the focus being on the prevention of accidents and infection.
- **1961 Preschool playgroup movement starts** – London mother, Belle Tutaev, wrote to the *Guardian* newspaper about how, in the absence of a state nursery place for her young daughter, she had set up a group of her own. The aim to offer part-time provision focused on learning through play. This was the start of the Pre-School Playgroup Association (now known as the Pre-School Learning Alliance).
- **1967 *The Plowden Report*** is the unofficial name for the 1967 Report of the Central Advisory Council for Education (England) into Primary Education. The report was called *Children and their Primary Schools* and was named after the chair of the Council, Lady Bridget Plowden (1910–2000). It observed that new skills were needed in society, stating that *the qualities needed in a modern economy extend far beyond skills such as accurate spelling and arithmetic. They include greater curiosity and adaptability, a high level of aspiration, and others which are difficult to measure* (Plowden, 1967).
- **1972 *Framework for Expansion*** – A White Paper outlining a 10-year programme for educational improvement which included a new nursery programme.
- **1973 Education Act** – Raised the school leaving age to 16.
- **1988 Education Act** – Introduced The National Curriculum. It made all education the same for state-funded schools, ensuring that all pupils had access to a basic level of education. Maths, English, science and some form of religious education became compulsory.
- **1989 Children Act** reformed the law relating to children and has been described as: *The most comprehensive and far reaching reform of child law that has come before parliament in living memory* (Herbert, 1993, p207). The principles of the Children Act were to bring together laws relating to children, public and private law, and the duties of local authorities towards children both in care and in the community. The aims of the Act were to provide a balance of power between families and the state, to protect families from inappropriate state intervention and to emphasise the role of local authorities in supporting families in difficulty and to reinforce the role of the parent when children are in local authority care, thus promoting the concept of *parental responsibility*. The Act also extended the regulatory system for Early Years and childminders.
- **1989 United Nations Convention on the Rights of the Child** was adopted in the UK and was fundamental to the inclusion of children's rights as a key theme within Early Years policy development.
- **1990 Rumbold Report** – The report into the quality of the educational experience offered to three- and four-year-olds.
- **1994 Code of Practice for Special Educational Needs** published.
- **1998 National Childcare Strategy** – Until the National Childcare Strategy there was no formal policy or structure for Early Years; at this time Early Years services came under the jurisdiction of local authorities.

- **2003** *Every Child Matters* – introduced following the Laming Inquiry. Designed to reform the whole system of children's services, a challenging programme of reform as it required the integration of a range of services.
- **2004 The Ten Year Childcare Strategy** – The government's ten-year strategy, *Choice for Parents: The Best Start for Children*, is the vehicle for taking forward and implementing the Every Child Matters agenda.
- **2004 The Children Act** is the legislative spine for the reforms, supporting a sharper focus on safeguarding children, with statutory Local Safeguarding Children Boards replacing the current Area Child Protection Committees and a duty on all key agencies to safeguard and promote the welfare of children. The overall aim is to encourage integrated planning, commissioning and delivery of services, and to improve multi-disciplinary working. Local authorities will work with other services through children's trust arrangements to agree local priorities for improving services for children, young people and parents.
- **2006 Childcare Act** – provides the first legislative framework for children from birth to five, to support children's care, learning and development.
- **2007 Children's Plan** – sets out the government's continuing agenda to keep policy relating to children and families prominent, with the aim of making *England the best place in the world for children and young people to grow up* (DCSF, 2007, p1).
- **2008 Early Years Foundation Stage** framework implemented.

ACTIVITY

Reflect on the timeline and identify similarities and differences between historic and current practice.

Conclusion

The history of childcare provision and education is linked to the economy and the development of women in the workforce, the change in family dynamics and geography, and as such the need for childcare provision outside of the family.

Having considered the history of Early Years provision, it is clear to see similarities in the work of previous governments and generations. The priority for children today is still, as it was many years ago, to eradicate poverty and improve educational opportunities and life chances for children.

> *Children are not incomplete adults; their current quality of life is as important as the future adults they will become.*
>
> (Dunn and Layard, 2009, p153)

ACTIVITY

Consider the key factors influencing childcare provision and education:

- religion;
- economic development;
- family;
- society – social responsibility.

How does each factor impact on practice and outcomes for children? Think about the impact of each factor within your own workplace.

CHAPTER SUMMARY

- This chapter has explored the historical background to the policies and legislation relating to children today.
- It has also asked you to consider how things have changed over the years.

The next chapter looks at the study skills you will be asked to develop and use while studying for your degree. It doesn't matter whether your specialism is Early Years or the whole of childhood; you will need to know how to make the best use of the methods discussed in this chapter.

REFERENCES

Aries, P (1962) *Centuries of Childhood, A Social History of Family Life*. London: Jonathan Cape.

Baldock, P, Fitzgerald, D and Kay, J (2009) *Understanding Early Years Policy*. 2nd edition. London: Sage.

Barnardos (www.barnardos.org.uk) (accessed 12 November 2009).

Cunningham, H (2006) *The Invention of Childhood*. London: BBC Books.

DCSF (Department for Children, Schools and Families) (2004) *Ten Year Strategy Choice for Parents Best Start for Children* www.dcsf.gov.uk/everychildmatters/earlyyears/surestart/aboutsurestart/strategy/10yearstrategy/ (accessed 5 January 2010).

DCSF (2007) *The Children's Plan: Building Brighter Futures – Summary* http://publications.dcsf.gov.uk/eOrderingDownload/The_Childrens_Plan.pdf (accessed 5 January 2010).

DCSF (2008) 2020 Children and Young People's Workforce Strategy: The Evidence Base www.dcsf.gov.uk/everychildmatters/strategy/childrenandyoungpeoplesworkforce/workforcestrategy/ (accessed 5 January 2010).

DfEE (Department for Education and Employment) (1998) *National Childcare Strategy Meeting the Childcare Challenge* www.dcsf.gov.uk/everychildmatters/research/publications/surestart publications/523/ (accessed 5 January 2010).

DfES Department for Education and Skills (2007) *Statutory Framework for the Early Years Foundation Stage*. Nottingham: DfES.

Dunn, J and Layard, R (2009) *A Good Childhood, Searching for Values in a Competitive Age*. London: Penguin.

Educational White Paper, *Framework of Expansion*, 1972 www.margaretthatcher.org/speeches/displaydocument.asp?docid=102233 (accessed 12 November 2009).

Herbert, M (1993) *Working with Children and the Children Act*. Leicester: The British Psychological Society.

Laming, W (2009) *The Protection of Children in England: A Progress Report*. Norwich: Stationery Office.

Maynard, T and Thomas, N (2009) *An Introduction to Early Childhood Studies*. 2nd edition. London: Sage.

NSPCC (National Society for Prevention of Cruelty to Children) www.nspcc.org.uk (accessed 12 November 2009).

Plowden, B (1967) *The Plowden Report: Children and their Primary Schools*. London: Stationery Office.

Herbert, M (1993) *Working With Children and the Children Act*. Leicester; The British Psychological Society.

Schaffer, R (2008) *Child Psychology*. Oxford: Blackwell.

FURTHER READING

Aries, P (1962) *Centuries of Childhood, A Social History of Family Life*. London: Jonathan Cape.

Cunningham, H (2006)*The Invention of Childhood*. London: BBC Books.

Nutbrown, C, Clough, P and Selbie, P (2008) *Early Childhood Education History, Philosophy and Experience*. London: Sage.

Pugh, G and Duffy, B (2009) *Contemporary Issues in The Early Years*. 50th edition. London: Sage.

Smidt, S (2006) *The Developing Child in the 21st Century*. Abingdon: Routledge.

3 EARLY YEARS STUDY

CHAPTER OBJECTIVES

By the end of this chapter you will:

- recognise your own learning needs;
- have some knowledge of report writing and presentations;
- know how to start developing your portfolio;
- appreciate the importance of learning with your mentor in your setting;
- understand some research skills and methods;
- be able to get a balance between study and working, and see the learning potential of your time at work;
- be able to undertake a critical evaluation.

Introduction

Good study skills have little to do with being 'naturally clever'. They owe much more to awareness, strategies, confidence and practice, leading to an overall development in your learning.

The study skills needed for Higher Education are ultimately gained only through studying at that level. Study skills develop through mistakes, trial and error, practice, experience, reflection and feedback from others as you move through the different stages of your course. You will be surprised at how your thinking, language and writing skills develop simply through continued study.

However, there are some basic approaches that can start you off on a good footing, help you cut corners, and accelerate the learning process. This chapter outlines some of the key teaching methods you will encounter on your course of study at college or university.

Learning styles

A learning style is an individual's preferred way of learning. Your teachers will probably try to use a range of teaching methods so that they can accommodate all of the styles of the students they are engaging with. Although there is no evidence that using a particular learning method will give you better results, it may result in you enjoying the course more if you are involved in activities you find enjoyable. There are, however, some well-known ways of improving your ability to learn.

For instance, there is a Chinese proverb that says:

> *I hear and I forget.*
> *I see and I remember.*
> *I do and I understand.*

Therefore, it follows that if, for instance, you listen to a discussion about carrying out detailed observations on the children in your care and then you read a good example before carrying out your own observation you may be more likely to understand what information is needed and why. This is a good pattern to follow when attempting to learn anything in life, and indeed you will find that in the college situation students are encouraged to research things for themselves rather than being given all of the information by the lecturer, as you may have experienced when you were a child at school. This is because it is now recognised that adults learn better by doing something to actively engage themselves in the learning process, rather than just taking in information relayed in a lecture. This often comes as a bit of a shock to students who have not studied for some time, and can be difficult to adjust to.

A number of educationalists have written about learning styles, in particular David Kolb has presented a useful model based on the Experiential Learning Theory (ELT) (Kolb, 1984). The ELT model outlines two related approaches towards grasping experience – concrete experience and abstract conceptualisation – as well as two related approaches towards transforming experience: reflective observation and active experimentation. According to Kolb's model, the ideal learning process engages all four of these modes in response to situational demands. In order for learning to be effective, all four of these approaches must be incorporated. As individuals attempt to use all four approaches, however, they tend to develop strengths in one experience-grasping approach and one experience-transforming approach. The resulting learning styles are combinations of the individual's preferred learning approaches. These learning styles are as follows.

- Converger.
- Diverger.
- Assimilator.
- Accommodator.

Convergers are characterised by abstract conceptualisation and active experimentation. They are good at making practical applications of ideas and using deductive reasoning to solve problems.

Divergers tend towards concrete experience and reflective observation. They are imaginative and are good at coming up with ideas and seeing things from different perspectives. These skills are particularly valued on courses where the students are studying part-time and working in children's or care settings as there is great benefit in sharing experiences with others and getting the opinions and different perspectives of the other students on incidents taking place in practice, which are then explored in class.

Assimilators are characterised by abstract conceptualisation and reflective observation. They are capable of creating theoretical models by means of generating ideas from their work experiences (inductive reasoning).

Accommodators use concrete experience and active experimentation. They are good at actively engaging with the world and actually doing things instead of merely reading about and studying them. Experience of teaching part-time, mature students indicates that they have particular strengths in this area.

Kolb's model gave rise to the Learning Style Inventory, an assessment method used to determine an individual's learning style. Individuals may show a preference for one of the four styles depending on their approach to learning via the experiential learning model, or they may have a range of styles that suit them.

If you research learning styles you will also come across Honey and Mumford's Learning Style Questionnaire; this was adapted from the above model by Kolb and the stages were directly aligned to the stages in the cycle and named Activist, Reflector, Theorist and Pragmatist. These are assumed to be acquired preferences that are adaptable either at will or through changed circumstances, rather than being fixed personality characteristics.

Many adults find that they use a combination of the learning styles, but basically an activist will prefer getting involved in an activity and doing something practical to help them learn; a reflector likes to observe and reflect on what they are seeing before jumping in and engaging in it themselves; a theorist likes to understand the underlying concepts and relationships before getting involved; and a pragmatist likes to get stuck in and 'have a go' at new skills.

Reflection

One of the skills that Foundation Degrees actively promote is reflection as a way of enabling students to improve and challenge practice in children's settings.

It is important that as an EYP, you are able to reflect critically on your practice in the setting. You might argue that we all reflect continuously on our work. Indeed, it is true that we often think about why something went particularly well or badly. But reflection on your practice should be a much more purposive activity; it involves a more methodical approach, often keeping a journal in which to write events down, with a view to ensuring you learn from the experience.

One of the most widely quoted definitions of reflection is that of Boyd and Fales (1983) who suggest that:

> *Reflection is the process of internally examining and exploring an issue of concern, triggered by an experience, which creates and clarifies meaning in terms of self, and which results in a changed perspective.*

This definition has similarities to that of Boud et al. (1985) who state that reflection is:

A complex and deliberate process of thinking about and interpreting experience in order to learn from it.

Therefore, the purpose of reflecting on your work is to help you to:

- make decisions based on sound judgement;
- link the theory you are learning in college to your practice;
- be better able to challenge practice and assumptions in the workplace, thus leading to more creative, satisfying and effective practice;
- develop the self-awareness necessary to help children in the setting develop their own critical thinking skills.

There has been much written about reflection but it has been generally agreed that through this process new understandings and appreciations may be acquired and problems reframed. Many authors write about three stages in reflection: first, the awareness of uncomfortable feelings or thoughts; second, critical analysis of those feelings; and third, the uncovering of new perspectives.

This is not to say, however, that you cannot reflect on positive events that may also prompt critical reflective evaluation and which some would argue are just as influential and more appropriate for use in analysing behaviours and making you feel positive about your own self-worth as a professional.

Schön (1983) has described reflection as the means by which the knowledge which underpins practice may be uncovered. He highlights the value of raising awareness of tacit or hidden knowledge. This could also be called instinct or intuition versus structured or purposive reflection.

ACTIVITY
Can you think of an example where you had a moment of déjà vu where you had an idea something was about to happen but had no idea how you knew that?

Benner, in particular, wrote about this in the field of nursing. She felt that practitioners built up a store of experiences over long periods of time working in settings that then allowed them to recognise patterns in events as they unfolded, allowing them to predict the outcome. Often, the person could not say how she knew what was about to happen but was usually correct in her thinking – this is often put down to a kind of sixth sense. Schön emphasised that professionals continually face unique situations, which they interpret in the light of previous experience, and he recognised the ongoing complexity and embedded reflection, in practice. In particular, he distinguished 'reflection-in-action' from 'reflection-on-action' (Schön, 1987), as follows.

- Reflection-in-action: thinking on your feet.
- Reflection-on-action: retrospective thinking or looking back over the event.

It is important that reflection on practice enables us to share our experiences and our solutions in order to learn from each other. Indeed, this is the strength of engaging in a course of study like a Foundation Degree because it allows the students to do this and to listen to each other's perspectives while offering positive feedback that allows one to improve the quality of practice.

This all sounds quite cold and clinical, but reflection also involves thinking about how certain experiences make us feel, and our own personal histories have a role in this. Being an Early Years worker, your instincts and emotions are what makes you the package necessary for the professional identity you aspire to. Chinn and Kramer (1999) elaborate on this *personal knowing* as the fundamental process of becoming a whole, aware self and of knowing the other as valued and whole. Personal knowing is enhanced when reflecting on the meaning of self in relationship with others. It is developed through the processes of opening and centring, and affirmed through response and reflection. Polanyi (1966) asserts that all knowing is personal, and that personal knowing includes a tacit and explicit dimension. Knowledge held tacitly remains hidden and develops into more explicit awareness as one engages in reflective thinking. Your Foundation Degree lecturers will attempt to develop this explicit self-awareness by encouraging you to share your experiences with others in the classroom.

It would be a shame, though, to engage in all this thinking just for oneself; one of the main purposes of reflecting is to improve the quality of your practice. Could it be that the process of reflection can also be used with children to help their problem-solving and analytical skills? Indeed, researchers recently found that preschool children thrive most successfully when engaging in activities that prompt deep thinking (Siraj-Blatchford, 2002). The research project, Researching Effective Pedagogy in the Early Years (REPEY) noted that environments which encouraged what researchers called *sustained shared thinking* between adults and children, fostered the greatest linguistic, social, behavioural and cognitive progress in children. Their work demonstrated that such engagement between adults and children relies on adults observing sensitively what children are engaging with and how they are exploring their world so that conversations with children are based on these. They showed that such discussions develop depth and meaning for all involved.

Other researchers have found that engaging successfully with children can provide and develop a powerful learning context where children's thinking is developed alongside their interests. Also, some research shows the importance of adults listening to children, and of children hearing one another. Their work emphasises how children develop knowledge and understanding within a social environment, and how that understanding is 'distributed' within a group.

So, in Early Years settings this means recognising how important our interactions are in children's development. Reflecting on how children interact and how we interact with them is a vital part of this. Thinking together could be seen as another way of sustained, shared thinking, itself involving a reflective approach as integral to effective Early Years provision (Miller and Cable, 2009).

You may find that your course leaders advocate the use of groups and discussion to facilitate reflection and there are a number of issues that may influence the success or otherwise of this. Many students on Early Years courses attended school when a more traditional approach to education was in place. They often find an adult-centred approach a challenge, causing a lot of confusion and conflict. Many students expect to be lectured and do not expect to do supplementary reading or to have to be self-motivated. Many students find the change to a more adult-centred approach very daunting.

> *I found it quite a big step for me really from my days at school which really didn't encourage you to think or question.*

> *This is more self-directed – it's adult centred, this is very different so that was a big hurdle.*

These expectations about how the course would be taught had obvious implications for how students would view group work where the facilitation style was unstructured and unauthoritarian. Many students may initially be confused by this style of teaching, though they do eventually adapt.

Previous educational experience sometimes leads to a continuing expectation that the teacher should take responsibility for the students' learning. Students frequently comment that even though certain learning strategies seemed to be a good idea, they would not participate in them or use them unless they were made to by the lecturer. Sometimes, students feel anxious about sharing their knowledge and experience for fear of looking silly. Dominant individuals who always give an opinion or advice could have the effect of silencing the other members of the group. Time is usually the key to resolving these issues – as students get to know each other and feel more comfortable sharing ideas, they feel more at ease with this approach.

Some suggested frameworks for reflection

Models vary in their detail and complexity. To take a very simple version as a way of starting to reflect you might try using the 'What?', 'So What?', 'Now What?' model by Driscoll (2000) as follows.

The **'what'** would be a description of what actually occurred. For instance:

> *The hall was set out for free choice activities with one adult-led craft activity: painting, sand, computer, trucks. bricks and boxes.*

> *Four children were working together and had moved all the boxes into one area and were stacking them into towers, counting and chatting to each other. A new member of staff came along and put them all back where the children had got them from. The children watched her, then got up and walked off. I went straight up to her and told her that what she had done was wrong as the children were really engrossed in what they had done and were working well together in an activity they had chosen themselves.*

This model would then go on to **'so what'**: an analysis of the meaning of this for you:

> *I felt so cross she had interrupted the game that I did not ask her why she had done this – but she told me later that she worried that the boxes might fall and injure one of the children; she also felt it was unsafe where it was situated.*

Finally, the **'now what'**: an action plan for how you would deal with a similar situation in the future:

I now realise I should have asked her why she intervened as she did before stepping in and then I should have explained why it was important the children were allowed to continue playing. I should have allowed her to explain before jumping in. I will try in the future to listen before I criticise others' actions.

As you can see, this offers quite a succinct way of recording events and the headings are so broad you really write as much as you like. However, some students like to have more structure and might like to follow Gibbs' (1988) cycle of reflection. This gives you more opportunity to explore your own feelings, which is an important and often neglected aspect of reflection.

CASE STUDY: A STUDENT'S REFLECTION

Studying for the Foundation Degree is really denting my confidence. I am unable to give as much as I would like to my family, my job and my studies. It feels like I am playing 'catch-up' in all three areas and not being successful in any.

In my professional role I have always used my spare time to prepare resources, research and familiarise myself with upcoming activities, prepare displays, rearrange the classroom: whatever it takes to perform my role to the best of my ability and for the good of the children in my care. However, with the extra time taken up studying and completing course work, the afternoon and evening session that takes me out of my setting and the knock-on effect this extra work is having on my home life, I find I do not have time for the things I would normally do. I am constantly trying to fit things in where I can. Thoughts are always running through my head of what I should be doing or what I have not yet done.

I worry that I am letting everyone down, I worry that I am not doing my job as well as I should be and that I might be judged badly because of this. Although I am keeping up with my studies it is hard work and challenging, which makes me question my own intelligence! I feel inadequate at home because my husband and our children are not getting enough of my time and when they are it's not quality – I am too stressed.

It seems like I am not performing to the best of my ability at work due to lack of time. I sometimes feel this is letting the team down, which is disheartening. The cause of this is mostly the time I am devoting to my studies. However, the advantage is that I am learning a lot to support what I do in the setting and am beginning to develop my role as a senior practitioner.

My own insecurity and lack of self-confidence is, I know, at the root of my feeling. I am managing to care for my family, carry out my professional role and keep up with my studies. I have always had positive feedback from my manager about my role within the team. The children in my care are happy and the parents are friendly. My role in the setting has developed over the years. I have more responsibility and, as a result, my job is more challenging. I need to take account of this when I am reflecting – I am working harder because more is expected of me. I have pursued a greater role at work and I am achieving this, which is a success in its own right.

I need to appreciate what I have done so far and understand that although the Foundation Degree is hard work, it is helping me to increase my academic skills and knowledge. Far from knocking my confidence I need to recognise that my ability at work has in fact grown.

The student writing in the case study above has used Gibbs' cycle of reflection. Here it is in diagrammatic form:

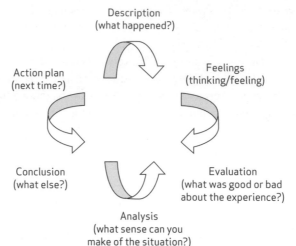

Figure 3.1: Gibbs' cycle of reflection

One of the problems of using 'a cycle' is that people often feel guilty or as though they are not doing it correctly if they don't move through each section before arriving at the final point. Perhaps, therefore, Ghaye and Ghaye (1998) offer a better approach that is based around a spiral where you can revisit the different steps and develop ideas as you progress from one part to the next.

It is important that students recognise the methods they use best to develop their skills, knowledge and understanding so that they can provide high-quality care for children through reflective practice.

Writing reports

There are few things more likely to put a student into a panic than realising that one of their assessments involves them writing a report. You may have just got used to writing essays so report writing may seem like a new concept entirely. Actually, you will find that it is easier than writing an essay because the structure of the report will guide you along each step. It sounds like such a dry task when you think of some of the Government reports on children or the childcare sector you may have read, but you need to remember that this is an academic exercise so your lecturer wants to see that you can be analytical as well as displaying all the necessary information in an organised way.

You may find this task is given to you as an assignment for your Foundation Degree, as it is a skill that is needed in order to share information about children in your care with other professionals. This is especially relevant when working in an integrated team with many other agencies, such as in a SureStart setting. There are certain formats you can use when writing a report. Here is one way of doing it.

Think about how long the report needs to be; it can vary in length as long as it meets the required outcomes. A report of one or two pages may be presented in memo format, providing a brief summary of activities. Longer reports will need to follow the structure outlined below.

Before preparing a report, it is important to clarify what information is required, and how much detail the person requesting the report needs. It is important to decide how many sections you are going to use to divide the report up into key areas and to give that necessary sense of formality. You should also have an idea of how many paragraphs will make up each section; ideally, there should be a similar number in each. The sections should be given headings that will direct the reader so they know what they will be reading about.

FRONT OF DOCUMENT

Section name and order in report	Section description and tips	Suggested order when writing
Title page	Title of report Author and author's name Person/organisation who requested the report Date of completion	7
Table of contents	Includes from summary through to appendices Does not include title page and table of contents page Uses the decimal numbering system (DNS) Indents each layer of the DNS Identifies appropriate page numbers	8
Summary	Represents 10% of the written report and includes: Why (the purpose of the report) Scope (what issues are covered and what issues are not covered) How (brief details of research methods) What (important results and findings) So what (major conclusions and recommendations) All covered in the same order as in the report	5

BODY OF THE REPORT

Introduction	What is the report about? Why is it being written? Any background information relevant to the report Scope (what will and will not be covered)	2
Discussion	Break your information up into sections and subsections using DNS Confine yourself to the facts Present your information clearly	1

Conclusions	This section answers the question: 'What does all this information mean?' Relate your answers back to the original purpose of the report Includes a clear summary of the main points Outlines your findings Do not introduce new information in the conclusion	3
Recommendations	Should be written in descending order of importance Emerge from the conclusions They should be honest, justified opinions of the writer and include: what is to be done who is to do it; how/when it is to be done	4
END MATTER **Bibliography** **Appendices**		6

Giving presentations

While studying for your Foundation Degree you will undoubtedly be asked to give some presentations. This is a valuable experience because it is something you are likely to have to do as a more senior practitioner. It also teaches you to be a good communicator, which is a particularly important skill when you are dealing with children and their carers.

Being good at presenting does not just happen; it involves a lot of effort to ensure that you have planned and practised it. It is not, as is often thought, a talent that some people have and others don't, but a skill you can learn with experience.

ACTIVITY
Think about some people you have really admired for their public speaking or presentation skills. What techniques do they use that you can add to your own repertoire?

Preparing your presentation

Purpose of your presentation

When you are presenting it is important to think, 'Why am I delivering this presentation?' Of course, we know you have been asked to do it by your lecturer, but the purpose is usually to display your knowledge about a particular topic or issue and to convey this to your peers. You need to be clear on the purpose of your presentation before you can write it, then it will be more effective. Just remember, you cannot tell your audience everything you know about a topic in the short time you may have – you have to limit it to some key and interesting or thought-provoking facts. In this way you are more likely to spark interest in your audience to go away and research the topic some more and to remember what you said about it.

Although you may know your audience well, it is important to think about why they should listen to you. What do you have to say that they would find interesting and valuable? You need to find out what they already know so that you pitch the level just right so they don't feel patronised or bored, and so they can understand what you are talking about.

Think of something that will really catch the audience's interest in the opening moments as it has been said that what is remembered are the opening remarks and the conclusion; what is presented in the middle is often forgotten so ensure you make an impact at the beginning. You can often do this, for instance, with a striking statistic that will shock everyone, or with a quotation. The use of humour, when appropriate, can also be useful.

Presentation structure

There are many presentation structures that you can choose from.

The most boring and ineffectual presentation style to use with a group of adults is the lecture method that many of us learned in school. The problem is that having someone talking *at* you is not likely to help you remember what they are saying. Some research shows that in order to retain information, it is important that adults are actively engaged in their learning, which will involve them actually *doing* something with the information you are giving them. This may involve you challenging them by asking them questions or by asking them to work together on some small group activity.

Question and answer structure

Another simple presentation structure that works is to run it as a question-and-answer session, although this may seem rather too challenging if you are worried you will not be able to answer the questions. A solution to this is to tell your audience that you will answer the most common questions you have heard about the topic you are presenting. Then you state the question and answer it. This is one of the easiest ways to give a speech. It sounds like a conversation and you will find it easier to remember. All you need to remember are the questions because you already know the answers. The best speech feels like a conversation.

Illustrating your main points

Ensure that your slides are clear and simply designed. Although it is tempting to show how many whizzy features you can incorporate into your presentation, they can detract from the points you are trying to make. Try not to put too much information on the slides if you have given your audience a summary of them as a handout; they can add points from the discussion as you expand on each slide in your presentation.

Bringing your presentation to life

Telling stories

Don't be afraid to use stories and anecdotes to illustrate and reinforce the main points of your presentation. Tell stories that create images in the listeners' minds. If they can see it they are more likely to understand and remember your message. The best ones are personal. Because they are yours, they are easier to remember and they make your presentation unique. We listen to stories. We hate lectures. The best public speakers are storytellers. The way to find personal stories that can be used in your presentations is to write them down; this is where your reflective journal could come in as particularly useful.

Rehearse your stories to edit them down into a short story that is easy to listen to. The hardest thing for you might be to leave out details. The hardest thing for your audience is listening to you describe unnecessary details. Just make the point and leave your audience to reflect on what you have said and to relate it to their own personal experiences.

Researching your presentation

Get your facts straight. Don't stand there saying, 'I think so' or 'I'm not sure'. Don't 'waffle' and pretend to know something you do not because your audience will spot that immediately. So spend time collecting and confirming your information. Too many public speakers are quick to present their opinions without providing clear substance. Avoid that trap.

Rehearsing and remembering your speech

The best public speakers do not memorise their presentation. Instead, know your topic and the issues, then make notes for yourself. But don't read your speech. That is boring. Instead, write key words that remind you of your messages. If you are using PowerPoint, develop some notes that you can print off as a notes page, that way you will have your notes under the relevant slides and you will be less likely to lose your place in the presentation.

Rehearse your speech on your feet at least three times. It is OK to rehearse parts of it in your car or sitting at your desk, but because you will deliver in on your feet – you rehearse the speech on your feet. It feels different when you speak on your feet. Get used to the feel of delivering your presentation and if you have a willing friend or partner who is prepared to make constructive comments, rehearse it in front of them.

The fear of public speaking

Studies show that our number one fear is the fear of public speaking. If you have a fear of public speaking or feel some anxiety, you are not alone. Even great speakers like Churchill experienced this fear, but he worked on his delivery skills so he could deliver even when he was nervous. Most professional speakers will tell you they experience stage fright. The fear of public speaking might be with you forever, but your audience does not need to know.

In most cases the symptoms of the fear are not noticeable to your audience. You might feel terrified but your audience doesn't know. There are several ways to overcome speech anxiety.

Focus on the success of your presentation. Before you step up to speak, take a couple of slow deep breaths. Speak slowly. Don't let it run away from you.

Delivering your presentation

Last-minute details before you begin speaking

Get the feel of the room and check the set-up before your audience arrives. This helps to make it your room. Walk around the room and organise the seating to suit you and your audience . Check your equipment and put on your slides to check for readability. Drink some water to both lubricate your vocal cords and hydrate yourself. Public speaking dehydrates you.

Your ally

Get one colleague on your side. This is a simple yet important secret to presentation success. This person should sit near the back of the room so they can survey the room, help late arrivers and do things without disturbing the audience. They will take care of the lights, handouts, ushering people to their seats and even asking a planted question. It is their job to head off problems before they erupt.

Eye contact

Talk directly to people. The best presentation is delivered as a conversation to every person in your audience one person at a time. If you want to be believed, talk to every individual, looking him or her in the eye. Don't make the big mistake committed by many novice public speakers of staring at the spot on the back wall. This one technique is a powerful element of successful presentation skills.

Emphasising key points

If you want people to remember something, repeat it at least three times during your speech. The first time they might hear it. The second time they might mull it over. The third time it might stick. *I have a dream* – do you know how many times Martin Luther King repeated that phrase in his famous speech?

Establishing rapport

Talk about things to which your audience can relate. Don't talk down and don't 'baby' them. To build rapport with your audience they must relate to you. Don't pretend to be something you are not, but show how you are like them. Be human. Expose a flaw. Show that you are not perfect. If you pretend to be perfect they will hate you and not listen.

Stay on time

This is one of the key things your lecturer will be keeping an eye on as she may have a number of students giving presentations on the same day, so start your presentation on time and finish on time. Do not repeat yourself for latecomers. If there is a small group at starting time, be prepared to 'start' with a discussion instead of your speech. Those who are there will believe that you started on time and those arriving late will seat themselves quickly, feeling a bit guilty for being late.

Finish on time, even if it means leaving something out. For that reason, always get your important message out early. Never keep the key message until the end of your speech. The audience might be asleep by that time. Position a small clock where you can see it so you know where you are in your presentation. Don't commit the sin of asking, 'How are we doing for time?' You should know – you are the speaker.

Look your best

Smile. You look your best when you smile. You look most trustworthy, friendly and confident when you smile. We do not want to listen to a speaker who is frowning. Don't grin like a fool all the way through your speech, though. Instead, smile before you start. Smile when you say something important. Smile when you end. Make it a warm, friendly smile. When you smile you look confident and help to improve the confidence of your audience. Smile.

Sounding your best

Drinking water before you speak will lubricate your vocal cords. Breathing deeply and slowly will allow you to project your voice and pause when you want to, not when you need to. Speak slower that you normally speak. The audience needs to hear what you are saying, think about it and internalise it.

Using equipment and technology

If you are using a computer projector and PowerPoint in your presentation, then avoid the mistakes committed by many presenters. Remember that these are supposed to support your presentations, *they are not meant to be the main focus of the presentation.* Ensure that your slides enhance your points. Create your presentation, *then* decide how to illustrate your points. You might have sat through some terrible PowerPoint presentations; that happens when poor speakers attempt to hide their lack of skills behind the use of PowerPoint.

Handling Q&A

Decide at what point in your presentation you want to take questions from your audience. If you feel inexperienced at presenting, it can be a mistake to allow questions throughout your talk as you may get sidetracked and forget where you are. Therefore, if you know you are only going to get questions at the end, you will be able to relax and deliver your presentation without interruption.

Finishing your presentation

End your presentation with a strong message. You can choose from several techniques. A call to action is one of the best endings to get your audience into action immediately after your speech. Other endings you can use include a rhetorical question, a positive statement, or a famous quotation. But *never* end with, 'Well that's all folks', which is an extremely weak ending. Instead, end on a positive action-generating note.

Balancing work and study

If you have not studied for a long time you may think you do not have the skills you need for advanced study, but you will probably find that your time-management skills are a great asset.

Often the most pressing problem is having to juggle work, study and home commitments. Make sure those close to you understand what you're doing and why. Let them know in advance your timelines and periods of greatest potential stress.

If you have already been managing home and work for some time, you can turn your time-management skills to a new set of tasks.

- Make a list of things that have to be done to keep life running smoothly.
- Make another list of things that could be done, but which are not really essential. They can be put aside till the end of term, or even reallocated to other family members.
- Do a backwards diary from your furthest deadline to the present time, so you can see how many days and hours you have available to allocate to study tasks.

College is a time for learning! Unfortunately, in attempting to study part time while working full time, as many Foundation Degree students do, it's hard to fit everything in. Often, the only way to achieve a successful work and study balance is to be more effective at studying.

The successful students are those who learn the most. Those who learn the most are those who receive better grades. Those who make better grades are those who are involved in their studies. The students most involved in their studies are those who accept responsibility for their own education and are active participants in it.

The next time you are in class, ask yourself these questions.

- What am I doing here?
- Why have I chosen to be sitting here now?
- Is there a better place I could be?
- What does my presence here mean to me?

And remember that you have chosen to embark on this course of study probably for a list of reasons that may involve testing your own abilities, developing your career, and also providing yourself and your family with a better income in the future. This makes you a very well-motivated student!

So here are some tips to help you learn more effectively.

- Never be afraid to ask a dumb question. The chances are that someone else in the group was desperate to know the answer but too afraid to make it obvious they didn't know already, and they will be grateful to you for asking.

- Use your lecturers. They want you to achieve well – it reflects well on them. It makes their work more rewarding to know that you are keen to learn.
- Don't sit at the back of the class. You, or whoever is sponsoring you, is paying a lot of money for you to be there so get the best possible value for money by sitting in the front and hearing every word. Reviewing notes for just five minutes after class can greatly improve your understanding of the session.
- Don't leave essay writing until the last moment; it won't help you to achieve good marks. Ensure that you study the material you are learning in college throughout the course, even if it is in short bursts; that way you are more likely to learn it effectively.

The truth is you will either control time or be controlled by it. The reason most students lose their handle on time is that they procrastinate. One of the major reasons that we procrastinated today is because we did it yesterday. Any large task can be divided into smaller, easier procrastination-defeating tasks. You too can tear a phone book in half – just tear it one page at a time! The bottom line is, don't make things harder on yourself by waiting until the last minute. Reduce stress on yourself by breaking up a large task into little tasks at a time. Don't wait until tomorrow to do it.

Developing your personal development portfolio

What is a portfolio?

A portfolio is a collection of samples of an employee's work, training and professional development, carefully selected and refined in order to show individual skills and knowledge. The contents are assembled in a three-ring binder that allows for simple, attractive presentation.

Portfolios are presented to potential employers to increase the chances of being chosen for a job. They are submitted when trying to gain entry into education and training programmes. They are used to document professional development activities. A portfolio is designed to reflect relevant skills and knowledge.

It is recommended that your portfolio includes the following information in the order listed.

- ❑ Cover Page
- ❑ Cover Letter (Profile)
- ❑ Professional Early Childhood Philosophy
- ❑ Résumé
- ❑ Licences/Certifications/Degrees
- ❑ Transcripts
- ❑ Job Descriptions
- ❑ Staff Evaluations
- ❑ Letters of Recommendation
- ❑ Outstanding Work Samples
- ❑ Individual Professional Development Plan Worksheet
- ❑ Five Year Professional Development Plan
- ❑ Professional Development Record

❑ Professional Development Reflection
❑ Professional Reading Record
❑ Professional Reading Reflection
❑ Professional Organisation Memberships

Optional:

❑ Professional Development Presentations
❑ Published Works
❑ Achievements/Awards

There is a growing interest on the part of employers who often ask to see a portfolio when they are interviewing candidates for positions of work with them. It can be a useful addition to the traditional recruitment interview to establish whether you have the knowledge and skills needed for the job. After all, it is a simple process for some people to sell themselves at face value, but if you can show that you have the organisational skills necessary to develop and maintain the collection of evidence your portfolio holds, it can only be an advantage over others less committed when you go for that interview.

Work-based learning

Work-based learning (WBL) is learning at higher education level derived from undertaking paid or unpaid work. It includes learning *for* work (e.g. work placements), learning *at* work (e.g. in-house training programmes) and learning *through* work, linked to formally accredited further or higher education programmes. Hence a learner may undertake a part-time, taught education programme, the focus of which is the direct application of learning to real work issues and problems, using projects and reflective assignments as the primary assessment tool. It is, therefore, ideal for Foundation Degrees in Early Years, or childhood studies, where students are learning to apply theoretical concepts to their practical day-to-day work and is a significant element of professional development and lifelong learning. It allows higher education institutions to recognise, assess and accredit learning from work at HE level. This fits with the ethos of Foundation Degrees by extending opportunities to adults who would not necessarily have engaged with further study, and thus contributes to widening participation.

It is likely, therefore, that the course you are studying has an element of WBL in its curricula. The format this takes varies from place to place, but it can be said with certainty that the work you do in children's settings will be an important aspect of the assessment of your course, where you will be expected to reflect on your experiences to demonstrate your knowledge of issues in the workplace.

Raelin (2000) has argued that WBL is different from classroom learning in a number of important ways.

- First, work-based learning is centred around reflection on work practices; it is not merely a question of acquiring knowledge and a set of technical skills (though these can be important), but a case of reviewing and learning from experience.

- Second, work-based learning views learning as arising from action and problem solving within a working environment, and this is centred around live projects and challenges to individuals and organisations. Work-based learning also sees the creation of knowledge as a shared and collective activity, one in which people discuss ideas and share problems and solutions.
- Finally, work-based learning requires not only the acquisition of new knowledge but the acquisition of meta-competence – learning to learn.

Assessment methods for work-based courses such as Foundation Degrees need to be tailored to a student-centred, problem-based approach. Hence, such methods may include:

- self- and peer assessment;
- assignments and projects;
- portfolio-building;
- presentations.

Each student will have his/her own learning objectives which can be facilitated through the use of learning contracts negotiated between the student, the lecturer and the workplace mentor.

ACTIVITY

Can you think of an example where you reflected on an aspect of your daily work with your peers in college giving you a new perspective on it? Or where you saw that the learning about the theory behind a skill you use every day gave you a new understanding of it?

Getting the most out of your mentor

A mentor should help the mentee to believe in herself and boost her confidence. A mentor should ask questions and challenge, while providing guidance and encouragement. Mentoring allows the mentee to explore new ideas in confidence. It is a chance to look more closely at yourself, your issues and opportunities, and how you can use your work experience to help you in your studies. Mentoring is about becoming more self-aware, taking responsibility for your studies and taking you in the direction you decide, rather than leaving it to chance.

What is a mentor?

A mentor could be:

- a term reserved for long-term relationships between people, one of whom is usually older and more experienced;
- a person selected by the student to assist, befriend, guide, advise and counsel.

Mentors are sometimes described as 'knowledgeable friends'. As with any friendship, this requires mutual respect and a commitment from both of you (Bennett, 2003).

The mentor has some key responsibilities.

- To get to know the learner and to foster a good relationship with the student conducive to effective learning.
- To agree some sort of timetable for meeting between mentor and mentee to discuss progress and issues
- To try to ensure there is a sound learning environment in which the student can reach her potential.

In order to achieve all these things the mentor needs certain qualities: trust; openness; mutual attraction; mutual respect; committment; energy; enthusiasm; empathy; patience; objectivity; assertiveness.

Of course, there are certain qualities expected from her student too: a mentee has to be open, willing to learn with a strong desire to do well.

The mentor's roles are many.

- Role model: image; beliefs; values; vision.
- Standard bearer.
- Coaching; teaching; facilitating; reflecting/analysing.
- Problem solver.
- Challenger.
- Supporter/stress reducer.
- Organiser/planner.
- Counsellor.

The important thing is that your mentor is someone you can go to when you are struggling with the academic demands of the course or when you are attempting to link what you are seeing in practice with what you are being taught in practice. Ideally, the mentor has been involved with studying in higher education herself and knows the difficulties of achieving a work and study balance.

CHAPTER SUMMARY

- This chapter has explored a large range of different study skills used by students in colleges and universities to ensure they learn effectively on their course.
- It has looked at some learning styles encouraging you to work out which style you use most effectively.
- It has looked at the key features of reflection and stressed its importance in improving the quality of Early Years practice.
- Writing reports is a key activity both in practice and on courses of study and this has been detailed in the chapter.
- Presentation skills have been explored.
- The importance of balancing work and study has been emphasised.
- Work-based learning and its usefulness for Early Years practitioners has been debated.
- The use of a mentor to help you with your work-based study has been discussed.

The next chapter looks at becoming an EYP and why it is important to do so. It asks you to reflect on your own role and it links that role to EYFS.

REFERENCES

Benner, P (1984) *From Novice to Expert; Excellence and Power in Clinical Nursing Practice*. California: Addison-Wesley.

Boud, D, Keogh, R and Walker, D (1985) *Reflection: Turning Experience into Learning*. London: Routledge.

Boyd, E and Fales, A (1983) Refelctive Learning: the key to learning from experience. *Journal of Humanistic Psychology*, 23(2): 99–117.

Chinn, PL and Kramer, MK (1999) *Theory and Nursing: Integrated Knowledge Development*. Philadelphia: Mosby.

CWDC (Children's Workforce Development Council) www.Children'sWorkforceDevelopment Council/howdoIbecomeanEYP (accessed 12 December 2009).

Driscoll, J (2000) *Practising Clinical Supervision: A Reflective Approach*. Oxford: Blackwell Publishing.

Ghaye, A and Ghaye, K (1998) *Teaching and Learning Through Critical Reflective Practice*. London: David Fulton Publishers.

Gibbs, G (1988) *Learning by Doing: A Guide to Teaching and Learning Methods*. Oxford: Further Education Unit, Oxford Brookes University.

Guy, P (2008) *Study Skills: A Teaching Programme for Students in schools and Colleges*. London: Sage.

Honey, P and Mumford, A (1992) *The Manual of Learning Styles.* 3rd edition, Honey: Maidenhead.

Kolb, DA (1984) *Experiential Learning: Experience as the Source of Learning and Development*. Englewood Cliffs, NJ: Prentice Hall.

Miller, L and Cable, C (2008) *Professionalism in the Early Years*. London: Hodder Education.

Polanyi, M (1966) *The Tacit Dimension*. Garden City, NY: Doubleday.

Raelin, JA (2000), *Work-Based Learning: The New Frontier of Management Development*. Englewood Cliffs, NJ: Prentice Hall.

Schön, DA (1983) *The Reflective Practitioner*. New York: Basic Books.

Siraj-Blatchford, I, Sylva, K, Muttock, S, Gilden, R and Ball, D (2002) *Researching Effective Pedagogy in the Early Years*. DfES Research Brief No. 356.

FURTHER READING

Buzan, T (2007) *The Buzan Study Skills Handbook*. London: BBC Active.

Peck, J and Cyles, M (2005) *Write it Right*. Basingstoke: Palgrave Macmillan.

4 BECOMING AN EARLY YEARS PROFESSIONAL

Excellence is an art won by training and habituation. We do not act rightly because we have virtue or excellence, but we rather have those because we have acted rightly. We are what we repeatedly do. Excellence, then, is not an act but a habit.

Aristotle

CHAPTER OBJECTIVES

By the end of this chapter you will:

- appreciate what it means to be an EYP;
- understand the reasons for professionalising the Early Years workforce;
- have learnt how to reflect upon your own role as an EYP;
- be able to link your role as an EYP to the EYFS;
- understand the importance of becoming an EYP.

Introduction

This chapter explores what it means to be an EYP, the reasons for professionalising the Early Years and how to use work experiences by sharing them in classroom debates and discussions. These debates and discussions will assist reflection, which is a key activity in vocational courses and within Early Years practice. For Foundation Degree Early Years students it is the basis of good practice. This chapter explains why reflection is important, how it links to work-based learning and practice, what it means and how to do it effectively. Throughout your studies the child should always form the focus of reflective practice and becoming an EYP.

The journey to becoming an Early Years Professional

Commencing your studies for an FD in Early Years or Early Childhood Studies marks the beginning of an extension to your own learning journey. Many practitioners have years of practical experience of working with young children and provide high-quality care and learning environments for those very young children. They already have a professional attitude towards their work, valuing and respecting the children, parents, staff and other professionals with whom they may work. The journey through the FD will result in a deepening of your knowledge and understanding of the learning styles and needs of the children with whom you work. It will also enable you, as students, to reflect upon your own practice when working in your teams, with parents, other professionals and during classroom debates and discussions, and to make strong links between theory and practice. Keeping the focus on EYPS, successful completion of the FD may give you the opportunity to progress to the third year of a related BA (Hons) degree and thence to gaining EYPS. For many, it will open a door that you never thought possible, and your knowledge and understanding of the Early Years will increase along with your self-confidence. However, in order to link the theories that will be learnt in lectures to your work-based practice, it is essential that you reflect upon all angles of your practice.

During a lesson on observing and assessing children a student stated that:

> *Since commencing this module my whole approach to taking observations has changed. They are much better and I am learning more about the children.*

Many of our students who have completed an FD have stated:

> *I knew children learnt through play, I now understand how and why. I can make links between theory and practice; the practice in the nursery has improved*
> *(Buckinghamshire New University course evaluations).*

These two examples demonstrate that continuous learning and extension of knowledge and understanding do result in improved practice, which is our ultimate aim.

Initially, it is important to establish what is meant by the title 'Becoming an Early Years Professional' and the different meanings it may have for you as Early Years practitioners. An EYP possibly presents differing visions to everyone; however, if like Aristotle we link it to 'excellence', it is acquired through training, repetition and having high but realistic expectations. Training extends our knowledge and, when linked to practice, consolidates that knowledge, enhances our practice and the experiences for the children in our care. Throughout this chapter it is hoped that you will all reflect upon these thoughts and your journey to becoming an EYP.

ACTIVITY
Think about the above statements and then write down a list of the areas of excellence and how this is delivered in your own settings. Discuss your experiences in small groups.

A profession

What is a profession? Using a general dictionary definition, it is a vocation or a calling (*Concise Oxford Dictionary*, 1995). Initially, one may think about professions such as architecture, dentistry, law, engineering, lecturing, medicine or nursing. These examples represent groups of people who have chosen to study to degree level and to belong to an appropriate professional/regulatory body such as doctors belonging to the General Medical Council. This can be supported by the following statements:

> *A profession is a group of people in a learned occupation, the members of which agree to abide by specified rules of conduct when practicing the profession.*
>
> (Quality Research International website, 2009)

or

> *An occupation, especially one that involves knowledge and training in a branch of advanced learning.*
>
> (*Oxford Paperback Dictionary*, 1979)

Boone (2001) states:

> *Professions are based on scientific and philosophical facts acquired through scholarly endeavour. Individuals who enter a profession do so for reasons that distinguish them from other work or vocations. They understand that their work renders a unique public service with a scientific or philosophical basis and/or body of knowledge that requires an extended period of academic and hands-on preparation. Professions are also based on specialised skills necessary for the professional to perform the public service.*
>
> (Quality Research International website, 2009)

These definitions of profession form a continuum of the opening quote from Aristotle, especially the need for ensuring excellence through training and then applying theory to practice. It is the aim of the CWDC to have an EYP in every setting by 2015 (CWDC website, 2009).

Therefore, the Early Years can be included as a profession in that it is a group of people who have decided to follow the vocation or calling to work with young children aged from birth to five years. However, before progressing further you must consider two very important questions to ensure that the focus of the child, within your studies, is maintained and that you maintain that focus in your practice and your journey towards becoming an EYP.

- Has the Early Years workforce always based practice on in-depth knowledge and understanding of the theories of development and learning needs and styles of very young children and has it been valued?
- Do we as a society value childhood?

The answers to these questions will be varied but sadly, there are many in the UK who do not value the Early Years as important, let alone the most important time of a child's life. This is despite research by psychologists, theorists, pioneers and scientists – including the writings of Plato, around 350BC; Comenius in the early seventeenth century and Rousseau in the eighteenth century; Froebel; Susan Isaacs, etc. (see the timeline in Chapter 2) – highlighting the importance of experiences that children aged from birth to five years were exposed to in order to fully develop. They recognised the importance of well-being, learning through play, outdoor play and the value of the family. Strong links can be identified between the theorists, the play pioneers and the requirements of the EYFS framework (2008). Loreman (2009) also found strong links when quoting Richards, Shipley, Fuhrer and Wadsworth (2004) who describe childhood as a *unique* stage of life when children are learning at an astonishing rate, and Molland (2004), Sprung (2003) and Vygotsky (1978) as a time when the world becomes an experimental laboratory with learning and the construction of knowledge occurring through play.

Persons who have not studied the Early Years still perceive working with very young children as an 'easy option' – 'you just play with them'. This is an opinion that is *not* held by those who do care for and educate very young children but it is often stated when young people are making their career choices. The fact that childcare and education is not easy was referred to on several occasions by Sally Featherstone during a conference on the implementation of the EYFS framework organised by Reading University (2009). Repeatedly it was stated, *nobody said it was going to be easy*.

Given that research supports the importance of the earliest experiences for children, it is imperative that the standards of childcare and education are raised in every setting through the professionalisation of the Early Years workforce. Government legislation and strategies for the Early Years sets out this vision through:

- *Every Child Matters* (2003);
- *Ten Year Childcare Strategy – the 'Children's Plan'*, 2007;
- the aims of the CWDC.

The CWDC is committed to raising the standards for all children in Early Years settings. Stating that:

> *a graduate-led profession is crucial to ensuring the best possible outcome for our children . . .*

it aims to have:

> *an Early Years Professional in every full daycare setting by 2015 and in every Children's Centre by 2010.*

(CWDC website, 2009)

A professional

What is a professional? How does one become a professional?

Your next task is to explore, in general terms, what is meant by 'professional' and then link this to the Early Years. Becoming an EYP is, as already stated above, linked to qualifications and knowledge, degrees and careers that lead to high standards of practice; in other words, lifelong learning/continuing professional development and disseminating this knowledge through leadership and support to one's staff (Brookson, 2010). Once in-depth knowledge can be demonstrated through raised levels of qualification, improved links between theory and practice, and the resultant enhanced experiences for the children and their parents in Early Years settings, then there will be an acknowledgement of the increased expertise of all who are involved. Early Years workers will be recognised as 'professionals' and experts in their field of work.

Here are some definitions of 'professional', from various sources:

- *engaged in a profession or engaging in as a profession or means of livelihood; 'the professional man or woman possesses distinctive qualifications*;
- *a person engaged in one of the learned professions*;
- *an athlete who plays for pay*;
- *master: an authority qualified to teach apprentices*.

wordnetweb.princeton.edu/perl/webwn (accessed 5 January 2010)

- *a person who belongs to a profession*;
- *a person who earns his living from a specified activity*;
- *an expert*;
- *of, pertaining to, or in accordance with the standards of a profession*.

en.wiktionary.org/wiki/professional (accessed 5 January 2010)

- *relating to or belonging to a profession*;
- *worthy of or appropriate to a professional person*.

(*Concise Oxford Dictionary*, 1999, p1141)

ACTIVITY

Now you have focused on the meanings of the words 'profession' and 'professional', would your thoughts about areas of excellence within your setting be the same as they were for the activity earlier in the chapter (see p44)? Re-write your list and discuss your thoughts in small groups. Are the children experiencing excellence or would extension of your own knowledge and development of reflective practice result in improved provision?

ACTIVITY

Write down the personal qualities an EYP should possess.

Consider the following.

- Do you have any member of staff who possesses all of these qualities?
- Are they all possessed within your team?

Reflective practice

Reflection was explored in Chapter 3 as a tool to improve our learning and reflective practice, which as all registered settings are aware, is an integral part of the EYFS. For example, it states:

The role of the practitioner is crucial in:

- *observing and reflecting on children's spontaneous play';*
- *building on this by planning and resourcing a challenging environment which:*
  - *supports and extends specific areas of children's learning*
  - *extends and develops children's language and communication in their play.*

(DCFS, 2008, p7)

Many FDs are written to include the requirements of the EYFS and will, therefore, include the requirement for you to write reflective logs, journals or diaries. Reflective practice, along with your deepening knowledge of childcare and education gained through your studies, should result in improved practice and improved responses to the individual needs of the children within your settings. The EYFS (2008, p9) states that: *well-qualified and experienced staff understand and engage in informed reflective practice.*

In this chapter you have already been asked to think about the words 'profession' and 'professional' and to link these words to the excellence of provision in your settings. This should have enabled you to think about your setting, to reflect upon the provision, perhaps the opportunities to improve provision, the need to continue to study and to discuss these points with your colleagues/peers. One could go as far as saying that all good Early Years workers *do* reflect upon their practice, but, until the implementation of the EYFS, was the process formalised so that, for example, there was a strong recorded link within the planning cycle of observation, assessment, planning, implementation and evaluation? This example is obviously planning for play and learning; however, reflection in Early Years should cover all aspects of provision, from the physical environment both indoor and outdoor for staff, children, parents, other professionals and visitors, through to resources, human resources, management, risk assessment and policy development. David Schön (1983) in his writings on the 'reflective practitioner' speaks about *reflection-in-action*, which has been described as 'thinking on our feet' reflection as we are working. Is this the type of reflection that has been used in the past rather than *reflection-on-action*, which is reflection at a later time, when there is time to analyse and share the reflective process, or is a combination of both used? It is often stated by Early Years workers, teachers, parents and others, that they have to have the ability to 'think on their feet'. In contrast, Kolb, presented by Arnold (2005) and Tindal (2006) was more specific about the process in that the person is involved in an **experience**, **reflects** upon that experience, thinks about the impact that the actions might have had and what needs to change, **conceptualises**, and then **plans** for change.

For further information on reflection/reflective practice and keeping a reflective log, see Chapter 3.

3. Conceptualisation:
What does it mean?

4. Planning:
What will happen next?
What do you want to change?

2. Reflection:
What did you notice?

1. Experiencing:
Immersing yourself in the task

Figure 4.1: Kolb's model of reflective practice

ACTIVITY

Think about and identify an example of reflection that you have been involved in, in your setting. Did this reflection have a positive effect on your practice? Now use the Kolb cycle to reflect on the same situation, discuss in your groups. Do you think the outcomes for practice would have been enhanced?

The importance of being reflective practitioners and experts within the Early Years workforce can be directly linked to the experiences provided for the children, child development, responses to individual needs and the importance of working with parents, as a team and collaboratively with other professionals. The Early Years is a time when the development of the brain is at its most rapid. Blakemore and Frith (2005) speak about the fact that a baby is born with approximately 100 billion brain cells. The EYFS (2009) states that 90 per cent of a child's neural connections in the brain are made by the time they are five years old. If these connections are not made, then many of the brain cells die. This demonstrates the importance of the role of the EYP when working with parents, multi-professionals and providing for the individual needs of each child, and is reinforced by a question and statement from the Early Years Professional Status:

Did you know that 90% of a child's brain connections will be made by the time they are five?

That means that their development and learning from birth to the age of five has a significant influence on their future lives.

(www.cwdcouncil.org.uk/eyps)

You, as EYP, therefore, have an enormous responsibility for each child (and their parents) who attends your setting, to meet their individual care needs and support their learning and development on their journey to achieving their full potential.

That's why we need the best people to help them develop and why CWDC and our partners have created the Early Years Professional Status (EYPS).

(www.cwdcouncil.org.uk/eyps)

When everyone involved with a child responds appropriately to their individual needs, they are supporting the all-round development of the child and supporting them to achieve the five outcomes of ECM to:

- be healthy;
- stay safe;
- enjoy and achieve;
- make a positive contribution;
- achieve economic well-being.

Throughout your journey towards becoming an EYP and in your future practice it is essential to use your developing skills of reflective practice and WBL in your settings so that the five outcomes of ECM are included in the everyday management.

As pointed out in Chapter 2, after the consultation process of the ECM Green Paper (2003) the following Acts and strategies were developed:

- the Children's Plan 2007, a ten-year strategy;
- the Children Act 2004, which is used in conjunction with the Children Act 198;
- the Child Care Act 2006.

These Acts, along with the EYFS framework, provide the statutory framework in which we work.

The CWDC was set up with the remit to improve outcomes for children and young people. Part of this process is professionalising the Early Years workforce through the attainment of Foundation Degrees, honours degrees and ultimately achieving EYPS – in other words, a graduate-led workforce.

Your professionalism, your competences or skills will further develop as you deepen your knowledge and understanding of children's development and learning needs through study, observation, planning and regular reflection on and documentation of your practice. Dahlberg et al. (2007) speak about pedagogical documentation as a way of revisiting and reviewing earlier experiences that can help one to learn from past experience and influence future practice.

> *This presupposes, however, that pedagogues engage in continuous self-reflection, something which poses high requirements on the professionalization, but something which also can function as a challenge and inspiration for a deeper engagement.*
>
> (Dahlberg et al., 2007, pp153–4)

Thus professionalism and reflection, it can be said, are inseparable!

Throughout your work in Early Years settings there is obviously the day-to-day organisation to be considered and planning for individual needs. This organisation will now be considered under the following headings, taken from the EYFS framework.

- Team working and working with other professionals.
- Working with parents.

- Safeguarding children.
- Ethical issues.

Team working and working with other professionals

Team working

With the experience you, as Early Years workers, have had prior to commencing study for your FD, you will already be aware of the importance of team working within your settings and working collaboratively with other professionals from outside agencies. The learning outcomes and all-round progression for children requiring intervention for learning or for health is very positive when multi-professionals work together. Conversely, when staff and/or multi-professional teams do not work together the journey forward, for the child and adults directly involved with that child, is not so positive. This is supported by Moss and Petri (2002) during research into children's spaces, while in Sweden they found that although in some instances there were problems with teamwork, where there was a strong team there was debate and rethinking *about different professional cultures and images of the child*. They also speak about including the children in the planning for the setting.

As an EYP you will be expected to lead and manage teams even if you are not directly involved in management at this time. The size of teams will vary greatly, dependent upon the setting. There are two examples to be considered here.

- Day care – the size of the teams working with the different age groups depends upon the number of children the setting is registered to admit and the child/adult ratios required for the different age groups, but could have at least four members of staff in each room.
- School Reception class – may have one teacher and a teaching assistant.

In both instances, these rooms form part of a larger organisation, a larger team that will also have influences upon the practice in each area/classroom.

ACTIVITY

Consider the two settings above. How would you ensure that strong teams are developed within their immediate context and then within their organisations?

When working in teams it is important to consider the roles and expertise of all members and to identify areas for continuing professional development (CPD). Good team managers and leaders:

- value and respect the contributions of their staff;
- listen as well as inform;
- include all staff in decision making and development of policies;
- manage changes that will arise in all settings;
- provide effective methods of open communication;
- have a vision for future development and provision;
- maintain focus on the task being considered;

- are able to make decisions when necessary;
- identify training needs;
- lead their team forward.

Belbin (2006), cited in Paige-Smith and Craft (2008), had five principles for effective team performance:

1. *A clear set of team objectives to be performed by each team member, whose status will depend on their (a) professional knowledge and (b) individual way of interacting within a team.*
2. *A balance of team members and roles in relation to the task required.*
3. *A recognition of how each team member can contribute to the team.*
4. *Some team members being more able to carry out certain tasks.*
5. *A range of different team members with different types of expertise.*

(Paige-Smith and Craft, 2008, p37)

Good communication is the key to strong teams, sharing information, increasing knowledge and checking understanding with resultant collaborative working. Strong, informed teams are able to provide appropriately for the individual needs of the children for whom they care and educate.

One of the major changes for all settings involved with the care and education of children aged from birth to five years has been the introduction and implementation of the EYFS framework in September 2008. One of the main focuses of this framework is working in multi-disciplinary teams to ensure the inclusion of all children in settings. Many Early Years workers were, and still remain, very anxious about this change because they have been concerned about their ability to respond to the individual needs of children with complex needs.

Working with other professionals

Working with other professionals forms an integral part of working in the Early Years; many settings work closely with Health Visitors and Early Years Advisers from the local authorities. Other professionals may become part of the extended team with whom you work to ensure the best development and learning outcomes for each individual child. These include:

- dieticians;
- educational psychologists;
- family workers;
- general practitioners;
- occupational therapists;
- physiotherapists;
- safeguarding children team;
- school nurses;
- social workers;
- specialist nurses, e.g. asthma nurses;
- speech therapists.

Children's Centres may benefit from having many of the above professionals working together under one roof and providing different services in response to the needs of the local community.

Working with multi-disciplinary teams can pose concerns as well as benefits; one main concern is that the voice of the child may be lost. The child must always remain the focus and, where possible, be included in the team and participate in discussions, particularly when the decisions being make affect them personally.

How do we maintain the focus on the child when so many agencies may be involved in their care and education?

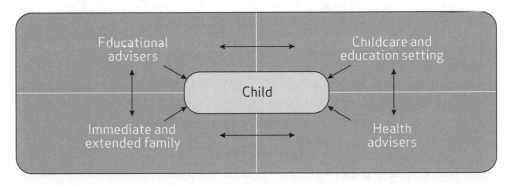

Figure 4.2: Multi-disciplinary teams working with a child

The benefits of working with other professionals in a collaborative, cohesive, educational environment have recently been highlighted in a report from the World Health Organization (2009), *Interprofessional Education*. One aspect of this is professions learning about, from and with each other to improve health outcomes. This can be adapted to apply to Early Years workers who not only educate very young children but also care for and promote the physical and mental health and well-being of those children. The Early Years workforce should be learning from, and working with other professionals, to improve the learning outcomes for children and to achieve the five outcomes of ECM.

ACTIVITY

Divide into groups of three or four, take two or three of the above professions, research their roles and your own role. Identify a child in each of your settings who requires multi-professional support and the professionals who may be involved. How can you learn from each other and how will you work together to ensure the all-round progression of the child? Reflect on the progress made to date for this child. How can the outcomes be improved upon or continuing progression be achieved?

Communication is the key to effective collaborative working, followed by respect for the specific expertise of each professional. Working with professionals such as those listed above will enable Early Years workers to:

• identify care and learning needs;
• develop individual care and learning plans for the children, as necessary;
• implement and then review the plans regularly, ideally with all parties present;

• continue to observe and assess the child;
• provide progress reports to support future planning.

When working in teams, Early Years workers must always consider and include the most important people in a child's life – their parents.

Working with parents

The term 'parent/s' will be used in this section of the chapter to include fathers, foster carers, guardians and mothers.

In order to work in partnership with parents it is necessary to understand and acknowledge their role. It is has been recognised and explained by Whalley (2007) and Ward (2009) that parents are their child's/children's first educators and that young children respond well in a setting when their parents are acknowledged and accepted by the staff. This is reiterated in the EYFS *Principles to Practice*:

> *Parents are children's first and most enduring educators. When parents and practitioners work together in Early Years setting, the results have a positive impact on children's development and learning.*
>
> (DCSF, 2008, Positive Relationships 2.2)

Parents are not only a child's first educators, before education they also, it may be said 'obviously', provide for the basic needs of the child such as food, shelter, warmth, love and care from the minute the child is born, until usually the late teens or early twenties. They work towards ensuring the health and well-being, and all-round development, accessing opportunities for recreation and learning, communicating and including their child/children in the culture of the family and community. Parents have a very important, time-consuming, emotional but ultimately an enjoyable and rewarding role. Therefore, working with parents to ensure that each parent is valued and that the knowledge Early Years Practitioners have of each child is as complete as possible should form an integral part of the philosophy of every setting. Dahlberg et al. (2007) explain that working with parents is not as pedagogues giving information to parents, but as a reflective analytic relationship which results in a deepening understanding on both sides – democratic practice not social control.

ACTIVITY
Consider when the communication with parents begins.

What important message should be conveyed to all parents?

CASE STUDY

Recently, during a visit to a drop-in session at a Children's Centre, as a carer, it became apparent, to the author, that a mother with two children, one aged approximately four years and the other a baby of six months, was not being spoken to or acknowledged by the members of staff. One of the other parents spoke to this mother asking how old her baby was, by way of creating an opening to include the mother and her children in the group; she replied briefly 'six months'. The parent then commented on the fact that the baby was very tall. The mother did not understand the comment, she shrugged and smiled, so sign language was used. There was another mother who spoke to her very briefly but otherwise no notice was taken. Not one member of staff made an attempt to speak to her or her children.

ACTIVITY

What constraints could there have been that prevented communication, other than the language barrier?

As a manager how would you reflect upon this situation?

How would you manage a situation such as this in the future?

Could a situation such as this have arisen in your setting?

Working with parents and forming partnerships is not always easy, due to some of the constraints that you have identified when considering the above case study, and situations that may have arisen within your own settings. First impressions create a lasting impact.

ACTIVITY

Think about the following as if you were a parent who has telephoned a setting and arranged an appointment to visit.

- How did the person on the telephone reply to a request?
- Was that person polite?
- Were you listened to?
- Were you put at ease?
- Was the information pack received within the stated time, e.g. one week?
- Does the setting have access to interpreters?
- Were you and your child/children invited to visit the setting?
- Were you and your child/children made to feel welcome during the visit?
- Did you feel comfortable and at ease in the setting?
- Was/were your child/children spoken to during the tour of the setting?
- How were you greeted by other members of staff?
- Were the children engaged in their play and learning?
- Were the staff interacting with the children through shared sustained thinking?
- Did you like the setting and feel that you would like your child/children to attend?

Can you remember an incident when a parent you were showing round appeared really happy with the setting and one when a parent appeared anxious? What actions did you take? Did you reflect upon the incidents, create action points and act upon those action points? What impact did this have on your practice?

Following the initial introduction to the setting, the journey to forming a strong partnership with parents begins. Good communication is essential; a key person should be allocated or chosen by the parent and child to provide continuity of care and education, and form the main link between home and the setting.

ACTIVITY
Reflect on the key person provision in your setting.

- Does it work well?
- Could it be improved?
- How can it be improved?

The appointment of key persons in the nursery has been included in the requirements of the EYFS. It is stated that:

A key person has special responsibilities for working with a small number of children, giving them the reassurance to feel safe and cared for and building relationships with their parents.

(DCSF, 2008, p15)

During research undertaken at Pen Green (Whalley, 2001), it became very apparent that parents did have the advantage of prior knowledge of their child, their development and experiences, as well as acting as interpreters for children, especially those aged two to three years who would be attempting to tell a member of staff about, for example, a family outing.

The formation of strong, positive partnerships with parents is very rewarding for parents and invaluable for the children and staff. It adds value to the setting because many parents bring expertise, experiences and cultures that can enhance and add to the resources and experiences of the children that are not necessarily already available. However, some parents, perhaps because they have had negative experiences as children while at school, feel intimidated when entering schools and Early Years settings or any formal setting. Early Years professionals should use all of their powers of gentle persuasion by providing opportunities for informal meetings. An area can be created, as present in many Children's Centres, for parents to drop in and have cup of coffee while their child/children is/are attending the setting or a drop-in session for parents and children to attend together. Use gentle encouragement to join in, to meet other parents and feel that they belong to a group. Isolation can be an enormous barrier to overcome; it may have developed for different reasons such as post-natal depression, living in an isolated area or feeling unwanted. For example, 'fathers', as described by Whalley (2001), who feel they are entering a female-dominated area; ill health; a recent move to the area from a different part of the UK or from abroad. Parents who have arrived from abroad may present communication difficulties because of language and cultural differences that must be taken into consideration and responded to appropriately. Siraj-Blatchford and Clarke (2000), cited in MacNaughton (2003), suggest that in order to work with families with diverse cultural and language backgrounds it is important to have knowledge of:

- *family history;*
- *religious beliefs and practices;*
- *children's everyday experiences at home;*
- *language practices;*
- *parent's theories about learning;*
- *parent's views on early education and schooling;*
- *community events and contacts;*
- *areas of expertise.*

Settings that value parents as partners already work in this way and gain most of the above information. Perhaps the areas that might not be included are religious beliefs and practices, and language practices. However, it could be argued that in our current society with many variations of family structure, this information should be gathered from all parents and seen as good practice. A reflection within Elfer et al. (2003) poses the question:

> *Is it right that we teach our children our way (culture/family style or values), or should we think about other ways more matched to their home lives?*

(Elfer et al., 2003, p49)

Good practice includes home visits by the key persons to improve partnerships with parents and to observe children in the home setting. The observations of children in their own home are then combined with those taken in the setting to inform planning for the individual child. Again, this has to be approached in a sensitive manner because, as you know, some parents can feel that they are being judged. Parents can be encouraged to take their own observations and photographs, and to share these with the setting to identify developmental progress observed at home and family celebrations that can be discussed with the child. Parents and children will then feel valued, the self-esteem of the child will be raised and learning should be facilitated.

The above paragraphs and activities provide information to promote reflection upon your own practice when working with parents and the use of key persons in the nursery. They should have provoked thoughts about you yourself becoming an EYP and influencing practice within your setting. You will be involved in influencing policy and practice, ensuring that the five outcomes of ECM are included in your practice and that the statutory framework of the EYFS is followed. This became mandatory for all settings registered with Ofsted in September 2008 and for many settings has been very positive. However, some Early Years professionals, including those delivering the Steiner Waldorf approach to Early Years education, have opposed some aspects of the EYFS, particularly those related to literacy and numeracy. For further detailed information see: www.savesteinerschools.org and the 'Open Eye Campaign'.

The formation of strong teams that include other professionals, parents and children will enable settings to achieve all five outcomes of ECM. This leads into the second outcome – 'stay safe' and safeguarding children.

Safeguarding children

Working in strong teams in the setting, with other professionals, in partnership with parents and within the legislative framework of ECM will help to safeguard children. It is the duty of everyone involved in the care and education of children and young people to ensure that children, as the second outcome of ECM states, 'stay safe'. It is mandatory to have a 'Safeguarding' policy and a 'Designated person' in every setting, and for every member of the team to be aware of and to understand the content of the policy and to know who the designated person is.

The Children Act 1989 states that:

The Welfare of the Child is Paramount.

It also states that there should be collaboration, co-operation and communication between all agencies involved in the protection of children. Despite this Act being in place, children continued to be abused, and, in cases such as that of Victoria Climbié, they died. Following this very sad incident there was an inquiry, led by Lord Laming. As a result of this inquiry, the government Green Paper *Every Child Matters* was published in 2003, out of which the Children Act 2004 became legislation.

The overall aim of the Children Act 2004 is to:

> *. . . encourage integrated planning, commissioning and delivery of services as well as improve multi-agency working, remove duplication, increase accountability and improve the co-ordination of individual and joint inspections in local authorities.*

The Childcare Act 2006 has been written specifically to address the needs of Early Years children, particularly those living in deprived areas. Local authorities (health and education), Sure Start and Early Years settings have a duty to identify children in need and those with special educational needs,

> *by ensuring early childhood services are integrated to maximise access and benefits to families.*

It also introduces the EYFS framework, which

> *will support providers in delivering high quality integrated early education and care for children from birth to age 5.*

> *and sets out the legislation for registration of settings with Ofsted.*
>
> (Childcare Act, 2006, Summary, DCSF website, accessed 14 January 2010)

The Children's Plan 2007 has a target to halve child poverty by 2010, eradicate child poverty by 2020, improve educational outcomes and improve child health. It also aims to reduce the offending rate of young people.

The Acts listed help Early Years Professionals to *safeguard and promote the welfare of children* and to develop high-quality provision, but do not mean that there will not be abuse. We have to be vigilant within our practice to ensure that our provision works towards meeting the five outcomes of ECM, as well as being able to recognise the signs and symptoms of abuse and the procedures to follow should abuse be suspected. We should teach the children to keep themselves safe and keep them safe through risk assessment and quality provision, including safe recruitment. It is also vital that staff attend regular 'safeguarding' training and updates in conjunction with reviewing the Safeguarding policy within your setting.

ACTIVITY

Discuss in groups the way you ensure that all staff are aware of and understand your Safeguarding policy.

How will you ensure that staff recognise and know when to report suspected incidents of abuse?

How will you ensure that children 'stay safe' within your setting? Discuss.

List the other policies that link to safeguarding. Do remember the widest remit of keeping children safe.

Whenever there is a horrific incident of abuse like that of Victoria Climbié and more recently Baby P, awareness and anxiety are heightened. While it is imperative to always be aware and to identify situations early, it is also important not to jump to conclusions because of these anxieties. Work together in teams and always seek advice from the local safeguarding team or social services. Plan age-appropriate activities that will teach children ways of keeping themselves safe and activities that challenge children's development and abilities. Work closely with parents, obtain their permission for their children to participate in these challenging activities, share risk assessments with parents and ensure that your staff are also protected.

The Statutory Framework of the Early Years Foundation Stage under section 3 – look under the Welfare requirements, Safeguarding and promoting children's welfare, specific legal requirements – states that a *Safeguarding Policy must be implemented*, and it lists the information that must be provided for parents, the information that must be provided by parents and that written records, including complaints, must be maintained (DCSF, 2008, pp22–3). Pp24–5 cover premises and security, outings and equality of opportunity, and pp26–7 cover promotion of and response to the health needs of children. These requirements support the last part of the above activity where you are asked to remember the widest remit of keeping children safe.

To expand on this still further, the importance of staffing should be explored. *Providers must ensure that adults looking after children, or having unsupervised access to them, are suitable to do so* (DCSF, 2008, p29). What is meant by being suitable and safe recruitment?

Providers should make decisions of suitability using evidence from:

- *CRB [Criminal Records Bureau] disclosure;*
- *references;*
- *full employment history;*
- *qualifications;*

- *interviews;*
- *identity checks;*
- *any other checks undertaken, for example medical suitability.*

Providers should notify all people connected with their provision who work directly with children that they expect them to declare to them all convictions, cautions, court orders, reprimands and warnings which may affect their suitability to work with children.

(DCSF, 2008, p29)

Providers also have to be aware of the new Independent Safeguarding Authority (ISA) scheme which is just being implemented.

ACTIVITY

Think about the above recruitment procedures. Do you follow these procedures in your settings? Discuss your recruitment procedures. Do you ensure that a new member of staff has a clear CRB check prior to commencing employment?

Other considerations linked to staffing (DCSF, 2008) are as follows.

- Qualifications should be checked carefully on the CWDC website. Some level 3 qualifications are not recognised. However, level 5 Foundation Degrees in Early Years and Early Childhood Studies are recognised by Ofsted and a person with such a degree will be recorded as a person with a level 3 qualification.
- Any changes of staff, changes to the name of the setting or any significant event likely to affect the suitability of the provider or any person working within the setting must be notified to Ofsted.
- Staff ratios must be correct in each area/room at all times, not just on the premises.
- Lists of policies are also included; however, Early Years provision within schools is not required to have separate policies for the EYFS.
- Within the safe and secure environments should be the opportunities for interaction, exploration and diverse learning and development.
- Regular risk assessments should be completed and regularly reviewed and amended as necessary.

Ethics

Throughout this chapter we have been reflecting on our practice, using observations to identify children's learning and developmental needs, working in teams, working with other professionals, working with parents and working within the legal framework of ECM and the EYSF. In order to reflect, to take observations and work in a professional way, our practice should be conducted using an ethical code of practice. Consider the following quote:

Above all, we shall not harm children. We shall not participate in practices that are disrespectful, degrading, dangerous, exploitative, intimidating, emotionally damaging or physically harmful to children.

National Association for the Education of Young Children, 1998

Would it perhaps be better if the above quote was written using positive language? For example:

- We will ensure the safety of all of the children at all times.
- We will show respect to all children, their parents and everyone we work with.
- We will use appropriate language, ensure that everyone is treated fairly, support the all-round development of the children and support the emotional needs of the children and their parents.
- We will form strong partnerships with parents.

ACTIVITY

Do you work within a set of moral principles and have a full understanding of the difference between right and wrong among the staff in your setting?

Now consider the four principles of the EYFS:

1. **A unique child** – recognises that every child is a competent learner from birth who can be resilient, capable, confident and self-assured. The commitments are focused around development; inclusion; safety; and health and well-being.
2. **Positive relationships** – describes how children learn to be strong and independent from a base of loving and secure relationships with parents and/or a key person. The commitments are focused around respect; partnership with parents; supporting learning; and the role of the key person.
3. **Enabling environments** – explains that the environment plays a key role in supporting and extending children's development and learning. The commitments are focused around observation, assessment and planning; support for every child; the learning environment; and the wider context – transitions, continuity, and multi-agency working.
4. **Learning and development** – recognises that children develop and learn in different ways and at different rates, and that all areas of learning and development are equally important and inter-connected.

(DCSF, 2008, p9)

The majority of Early Years' writings concerned with ethics are about ethical practice when conducting research. Farrell (2005) speaks about ethics being concerned with distinctions between right and wrong (Kimmel, 1998) and about conformity to a code or set of principles. As Rawlings (2008) points out, the four EYFS principles have inherent values that inform practice and the development of setting policies. The set of principles provide a sound basis for an ethical framework for the Early Years workforce to follow and enforce throughout their practice when working with children, parents, teams and other professionals.

In conclusion, in order to become an EYP, it is essential to reflect on your practice, increase your knowledge and understanding of children's learning and development, ensure that the child remains the focus of your planning and that you include the child, parents, your team and other professionals in the care and education of each child. Inclusion of the child in decision making does depend on the child being of an appropriate age to participate and on the decision to be made. However, do remember that very young children are able to make choices; they may only be a few months old but are capable of reacting to situations and through their cries, smiles and body language you know whether they accept or do not accept, for example, an activity or the food provided.

A final thought, on your journey towards becoming an EYP. How are you going to use reflective practice to make a difference to the experiences provided for the children in your setting?

Learn, reflect, extend your thinking, plan and raise the standards of care and education by meeting the individual needs of each child, parents and staff involved your setting.

We are what we repeatedly do.

Aristotle

CHAPTER SUMMARY

- This chapter has looked at what it means to be an EYP and it has explored the changing feelings and developing confidence of students studying for their Foundation Degree.
- It has defined 'profession' and detailed what it means to be a professional working in a diverse team before exploring the importance of reflection on that path.
- The chapter also stresses the importance of working with parents and families in ensuring an holistic approach to care.
- It has looked at how personal philosophies affect the way in which we relate to children, families, colleagues and other professionals in Early Years settings.

Chapter 5 is intended to help you to develop an understanding of the ways in which children learn and to appreciate the importance of the Early Years setting in supporting children's learning and development. It will enable you to link theory to the principles and themes of the EYFS.

REFERENCES

Brookson, M (2010) E-Learning: Using ICT to support professional development and children's learning, in Bruce, T (2010) *Early Childhood: a Guide for Students*. London: Sage.

Concise Oxford Dictionary (1995).

Dahlberg, G, Moss, P and Pence, A (2007) *Beyond Quality in Early Childhood Education and Care*. London: Routledge.

DCFS (2008) *Practice Guidance for the Early Years Foundation Stage*, Nottingham: DCSF Publications.

DCFS (2008) *Statutory Framework for the Early Years Foundation Stage*. Nottingham: DCSF Publications.

Elfer, P, Goldschmied, E and Selleck, D (2003) *Key Persons in the Nursery*. London: David Fulton.

Farrell, A (2005) *Ethical Research with Children*. Maidenhead: Open University Press.

Frith, U and Blakemore, S-J (2005) *The Learning Brain: Lessons for Education*. Oxford: Blackwell.

Loreman, T (2009) *Respecting Childhood*. London: Continuum.

Moss, P and Petrie, P (2002) *From Children's Services to Children's Spaces*, London: Routledge.

Paige-Smith, A and Craft, A (2008) *Developing Reflective Practice in the Early Years*. Maidenhead: Open University Press.

Rawlings, A (2009) *Studying Early Years*. Maidenhead: Open University Press.

Whalley, M (2001) *Involving Parents in their Children's Learning*. London: Paul Chapman Publishing.

Whalley, M (2007) *Involving Parents in their Children's Learning*. London: Paul Chapman Publishing.

WHO (World Health Organization) Report (2009) *Learning Together to Work Together For Better Health – Framework for Action on Inter-professional Education & Collaborative Practice*. accessed via www2.rgu.ac.uk/ipe/WHO_report_Interprofessional%20Ed%20Sep2509.pdf

FURTHER READING

Blandford, S and Knowles, C (2009) *Developing Professional Practice 0–7*. Harlow: Pearson Education.

Daly, M, Byers, E and Taylor, W (2004) *Early Years Management in Practice*. Oxford: Heinemann.

Jarvis, P, George, J and Holland, W (2010) *The Early Years Professional's Complete Companion*. Harlow: Pearson Education.

MacLeod-Brudenell, I (2004) *Advanced Early Years Care and Education*. Oxford: Heinemann.

Miller, M and Cable, C (2008) *Professionalism in the Early Years*. London: Hodder Education.

Reed, M and Canning, N (2010) *Reflective Practice in the Early Years*. London: Sage.

WEBSITES

www.brainyquote.com/quotes/authors/a/aristotle_2.html (accessed 26 October 2009)

www.cwdcouncil.org.uk/eyps/government-targets (accessed 26 October 2009)

www.cwdcouncil.org.uk/eyps (accessed 26 October 2009)

www.cwdcouncil.org.uk/integrated-working/leadership-and-management (accessed 2 November 2009)

www.dcsf.gov.uk/everychildmatters/about/ (accessed 14 January 2010)

www.en.wiktionary.org/wiki/professional (accessed 5 January 2010)

www.firstclass.ultraversity.net/~ian.tindal/rm/modeloverview.html (accessed 22 January 2010)

www.learningdiscoveries.org/StagesofBrainDevelopment.htm (accessed 27 October 2009)

www.qualityresearchinternational.com/glossary/profession.htm (accessed November 2009)

www.ssuclc.com/pdfs/ethics.pdf (accessed 14 January 2010)

5 SUPPORTING CHILDREN'S LEARNING AND DEVELOPMENT IN PRACTICE: DEVELOPING YOUR SPECIALIST KNOWLEDGE

CHAPTER OBJECTIVES

By the end of this chapter you will:

- have developed an understanding of the ways in which children learn;
- appreciate the importance of the Early Years setting in supporting children's learning and development;
- be able to link theory to the principles and themes of the EYFS.

Introduction

This chapter will explore the different ways in which children learn and how Early Years settings can provide appropriate support for that learning and development. Since the publication of the White Paper *Every Child Matters* (DH/DfES, 2004), the health, education and social outcomes for children have been high on the political agenda. It has been acknowledged that the early experiences of children impacts on their future lives and it is the responsibility of all adults to ensure that children are treated as unique individuals with specific needs and rights (DH, 2004). It is particularly important for children in organised Early Years settings that practitioners understand the individual developmental needs of children and have the appropriate knowledge, skills and attitudes to provide quality care and support for learning (DCSF, 2008). Cases of child abuse in Early Years settings have further emphasised the need for the monitoring of and appropriate training for all those working with children and young people (Morris, 2009).

Childhood can be viewed in many different ways in different parts of the world and in different cultures but the unique abilities of each child should be recognised in order that they may reach their full potential. The EYFS (DCSF, 2008) recognises this in four guiding themes.

- The unique child.
- Positive relationships.
- Enabling environments.
- Learning and development.

This chapter will explore each theme, expand on theoretical aspects and give examples of how Early Years practitioners can contribute to the health and well-being of children in their care.

The unique child

The *Every Child Matters* (DH/DfES, 2004) White Paper set specific outcomes for all children, that they should: stay safe; be healthy; enjoy and achieve; achieve economic well-being and make a positive contribution. Each child will have a level of competence and ability that will enable them to achieve these outcomes and these need to be identified according to their individual circumstances (Hall and Elliman, 2007). This means recognising that some children may need very specific help to achieve optimum health and well-being (Hall and Elliman, 2007). Early Years practitioners need to have a working knowledge of typical child development and good observational skills in order that these specific needs are met appropriately.

Children will reach developmental milestones at different rates and times, and a variety of factors will affect this, such as genetics, illness or disability, family history, or environmental factors (Herbert, 2003). Working in partnership with parents and other professionals is essential to identify problems early and offer supportive networks (DCSF, 2008). Listening to parents' or carers' concerns is important, but the ability to express professional concerns to parents can be equally important and challenging, and requires appropriate communication skills.

Children themselves also need to be listened to and respected, whatever their age and circumstances (Jones, 2009). Children may not always communicate their difficulties as adults expect, perhaps displaying types of behaviour such as frustration, which can be misinterpreted as bad behaviour or bad parenting: there may be an underlying problem that they cannot articulate.

CASE STUDY

Joe is 18 months old and is at nursery. Initially he settled quite well but gradually his behaviour towards the other children deteriorated and he became very disruptive, particularly during free play. He often sought one-to-one attention from adults and was more co-operative when there were structured activities. However, he struggled with following instructions and his speech was sometimes difficult to understand. The senior practitioner (Mary) suspected he may have a hearing problem and she arranged a meeting with Joe's mother who said that Joe had had a series of ear infections recently which had cleared up quite well with antibiotics. Mary suggested that a hearing test should be arranged for Joe to eliminate this as an explanation for his behaviour. In the meantime, a behaviour plan was agreed and the setting arranged to pay more attention to Joe on a one-to-one basis and ensure that instructions were clear and that he was facing them when speaking to him. A hearing test was done by the Health Visitor, and indeed, Joe's hearing was reduced in both ears due to a conductive hearing loss following the ear infections. Joe was referred to a paediatrician for further consultation.

Comments:
Hearing loss in children is a common cause of delayed speech and learning. Hearing problems are either congenital (from birth) or acquired later. A congenital hearing problem is usually associated

with a problem with the auditory nerve or the cochlea where sound is not interpreted by the brain. These children will normally be identified at birth through neonatal screening but children who have been damaged by infection in the uterus may not be picked up and the hearing can deteriorate over the first two years of life. Conductive hearing loss is extremely common and is usually associated with infection causing fluid in the middle ear, which affects the sound conduction through the ear.

Children with Down syndrome or cleft palate are more likely to have hearing problems than the rest of the population.

Children with hearing problems should be supported by the child health team and monitored with a view to referral to a Speech and Language Therapist (SALT) if necessary. Generally, children with conductive hearing loss grow out of the problem as the ear canal gets bigger but persistent problems can be treated surgically (insertion of grommets) (NICE guidelines, 2008).

This perceived 'minor' problem can significantly affect early learning and practitioners need to be aware of the processes of referral to resolve problems early (DCSF, 2004).

Positive relationships

There is an expectation that a parent will provide for their child in respect of their health, education, emotional development, nutrition, shelter and safe living conditions where they are able to do so (World Health Organization, 2002). Forming positive relationships that are secure and enduring are important aspects of child development, not just in terms of emotional and social development but also in the physical development of the brain (Gerhardt, 2004). Brain development begins before birth in the uterus where it grows in weight and forms potential 'pathways' called neurons (brain cells). Following birth, these pathways need to be joined together in order for an individual to function. These connections are called synapses and the connections are necessary to stimulate a range of processes enabling normal physical and psychological development (Horwath, 2007). In terms of learning, the brain has two neurological systems in place at birth: one is responsible for our reflex actions and vital functioning such as maintaining the heart beat, breathing and the sucking reflex; the other system is dependent on our external experiences (Horwath, 2007). The continuing growth of the pathways will depend upon the type of external stimuli that is experienced by the child; a young baby needs the experiences of touch, sight, sound, movement, interaction with adults and love (Gerhardt, 2004). Research on animals suggests that there is a 'window of opportunity' for the development of these pathways and this demonstrates how important the Early Years are in terms of learning, social and emotional development (Hall, 2007).

There have been cases over the years of children being raised in extreme isolation or deprivation and there seems to be little doubt that this will have an immediate impact on all areas of their development. There is, however, debate around the long-term impact of this deprivation and whether children can return to 'normal' following a change in their environment. With more sophisticated imaging equipment, we can now see areas of the brain more clearly and identify the areas responsible for language, problem solving, spatial awareness, co-ordination and our emotions (Gerhardt, 2004). This gives us opportunities to examine the physical effect of neglect on children who have been isolated or deprived in the first few years of life. The physical evidence suggests that there is damage to the orbitofrontal area in these cases and this will limit the ability to form positive relations and develop empathy (Gerhardt, 2004).

Early, loving attachments to another person have been explored as an important influence on the ability to form later relationships and also the ability to develop empathy with others (Schaffer, 2004). Supportive networks and relationships can help a child cope with the various developmental transitions they go through in their lives. However, recent evidence has suggested that children are more *anxious and troubled* in today's society than they have ever been and this makes it difficult to form positive relationships or networks (Layard, 2009; Unicef, 2007). Erikson suggested that life was a series of *psycho-social crises* that are inevitable and that the stronger the supportive, trusting networks are, the more successful transitions will be made (cited in Newman and Newman, 2009). According to Erikson, from infancy to two years old, the developmental 'task' is to learn to either trust or mistrust others (Martin et al., 2007). A study undertaken for the Children's Society, *A Good Childhood* (Layard, 2009), reported that in 1959, 56 per cent of people said that most people could be trusted; in 1999, only 29 per cent of people said that most people could be trusted. It also suggests that society has become more 'individualised', i.e. that the 'community spirit' is lacking and, without this, it is difficult to develop secure, supportive, safe networks with positive relationships (Layard, 2009). It is important for the safeguarding of children that they are able to identify for themselves a range of adults that they can talk to and feel safe with, and the *Protective Behaviours Programme* used in different settings is a useful resource to help children (and adults) to feel more secure in their relationships (Protective Behaviours, 2010; HM Government, 2004). The Protective Behaviours philosophy is to build the self-esteem and self-confidence of people in order that they make safe behavioural choices. This helps individuals throughout life to integrate confidently into society and avoid victimisation (Protective Behaviours, 2010).

With a secure and loving interaction with a main care giver early in life, a child is more likely to be able to move on to confident independence later (Schaffer, 2004). A safe base that enables children to explore and experiment for themselves allows for a growth of emotional competence or intelligence which prepares them for the highs and lows of life (Schaffer, 2004). This emotional competence describes the ability of individuals to understand their own emotions; a self-awareness of their strengths and weaknesses; and an acceptance of who they are (their self-esteem). The stronger the emotional competence, the more resilient an individual may be to cope with negative experiences (Lindon, 2007; Livingstone, 2008). As well as this, psychologists also suggest that self-awareness is important for understanding other people's emotions, being able to read other people's behaviour and be responsive to social 'cues' (Lindon, 2007). Social cues are about reading people's emotions, such as anger, frustration, anxiety, distress or sorrow, through body language, facial expressions, what people say and how they say it. It also involves having an awareness of people's personal space (Livingstone, 2005). Some children find this particularly difficult and unless they learn this, later socialisation can be problematic; anti-social behaviour has been associated with chaotic parenting style and this inability to emphathise with others (Respect, 2010).

This has been particularly illustrated in the cases of young children involved in violent crime, such as the Jamie Bulger case in 1993 and, more recently, the Edlington case of two boys aged 10 and 11 sadistically attacking two other boys, aged 9 and 11 (Norton and Norfolk, 2010). Cases like these stimulate discussions around societal expectations and whether Britain in particular is 'broken' (Cameron, 2010). Some suggestion of this is highlighted in the UNICEF report on the quality of life for children in 21 rich countries across the world, in which the UK was bottom (UNICEF, 2007). However, Socrates (469–399BC) suggested that: *The children now love luxury, they have bad manners, contempt for authority and show disrespect to their elders*. This perhaps is the earliest recorded concern about the behaviour of children in society. Today's society is illustrated by Libby Brookes (2006) who presents nine case studies of children growing up in modern Britain to illustrate the realities of their lives, giving real insight into their experiences; she also describes the creation of the concept of childhood.

ACTIVITY

Consider a child you have experienced in your setting who has had difficulty under-standing what behaviour is expected of them. How do they respond to the 'cues' of others (adults and children), e.g. disapproval, frustration, defensiveness, anxiety, being upset, etc? What can you do as a practitioner to support children who have this difficulty? How do you develop the socialisation process of children in your setting?

It is also acknowledged in *Every Parent Matters* (DCSF, 2007b) that both parents are important in supporting the developmental needs of their child. Fathers are often not acknowledged or considered in Early Years settings and this problem needs to be addressed by Early Years practitioners (Bruce, 2010). Given that since 1971 the divorce rate in the UK has continued to rise (Online National Statistics, 2010), and given the suggestion that the loss of a father figure is likely to impact on the early development of children and the formation of positive relationships, it is an area of consideration for Early Years practitioners. It is certainly an area that the Early Years worker will need to take account of if there is a change in the behaviour of a child in their care.

The key worker model within early years settings has a basis in the theories outlined above. Working with young children on a regular basis enables practitioners to identify specific need, form safe relationships and support learning.

Enabling environments: supporting children in practice

This section explores the responsibility of Early Years practitioners to provide an environment that supports all the developmental needs of the children in their care. Table 5.1 presents an overview of the stages of development from 0 to 5 years and the kinds of resources which are important to support each stage. This is not an exhaustive list and there is space in the table for you to add your own resources/thoughts.

It is argued that, as human beings, we need to have our physical and emotional needs met appropriately in order for us to maintain both physical and mental health and well-being (The Human Givens Institute [HGI], 2010). The Human Givens approach argues that there is a genetic blueprint, which has developed over millions of years, that is present in all humans and relates to the innate desire to have these physical and emotional needs met in order to survive

Table 5.1: Supporting learning/resources

AGE	LEARNING/DEVELOPMENTAL NEEDS	RESOURCES	YOUR SETTING
0–3 months	Safety, security, warmth, food, love (the human givens/Maslow)	Contracts with parents	
	Attachment	Safe handling/supporting head/sleeping on back/consider sudden infant death syndrome	
	Reflex actions: grasping, feeding, sucking, stepping or walking reflex, kicking	Safe feeding practices: sterile bottle preparation, etc. (consider issues around using breast milk)	
	With experience/stimulation: following movements visually, smiling, follows sounds with head	Provide safe stimulation considering all senses: vision, sound, touch	
		Babies also need sleep and rest times for growth; be aware of over-stimulus	
3–6 months	Independent head holding; size of the head grows along with brain growth	Consider safety: safe objects for practising grasping	
	Holding objects; hand–eye co-ordination improves, rolling over	Think about space for movement and co-ordination	
	Laughing, smiling, making sounds; developing language skills	Appropriate stimulation: think about sound, appropriate touch, visual awareness	

Table 5.1: Continued

AGE	LEARNING/DEVELOPMENTAL NEEDS	RESOURCES	YOUR SETTING
	Developing awareness of body – exploring hands, feet, mouth, etc. – starting to develop spatial awareness	Communication through body language, eye contact, baby massage	
	Awareness of others, faces, familiar carers, etc.	Also consider rest/quiet times/privacy	
6 months– 1 year	Weaning on to solid food.	Consider food: children should be having vitamin supplements at this stage and no added salt or sugar to foods, otherwise, at 6 months, babies can be introduced to most foods. Remember, children need calories for growth in the form of carbohydrates (includes full fat milk). Finger foods good for fine motor skills development. A 'free flowing' cup should replace the bottle to help with healthy teeth development.	
	Sitting, crawling, improving fine motor skills and hand–eye co-ordination		
	Making eye contact, interacting, copying behaviour, laughing, developing language		
	Developing sense of self; self-esteem and self confidence	Safe spaces for exploration and practising crawling and walking	
		Appropriate stimulation and opportunities for practising gross and fine motor skills and also socialisation skills	

	Tooth development		Full fat milk and dairy products essential for calcium
1–2 years	Standing, walking, balancing, improving fine and gross motor skills; self-feeding (finger foods)		Safe, large spaces and equipment for children to explore and experiment; involve children in making choices
	Spatial awareness		Consider learning through play: pretend play for developing social skills; sand and water: large building bricks; for sensory development, consider learning styles and provide a variety of choices
	Developing language and communication – speech development – mainly using nouns		Opportunities to practise words and learning objects – books and story times – makes connections between concepts
	Becoming more independent, sense of 'self', awareness of others, socialisation, etc.		Using games to encourage sharing
	Children learning through trial and error		Provide opportunities for allowing children a voice; circle times, etc.; show respect for each other, listening skills, etc.

Table 5.1: Continued

AGE	LEARNING/DEVELOPMENTAL NEEDS	RESOURCES	YOUR SETTING
2–3 years	More confident walking, running, spatial awareness, two feet jumping	Accidents common at this age – safe equipment and supervision essential	
		Provide a variety of play areas for children to choose and develop independence, including quiet areas with books, etc; good for children to start making choices decisions independently	
	Cognition and language development – making sentences	Be aware of children who have difficulties in socialising, communicating, concentrating or learning through their mistakes – may indicate: hearing problems, learning difficulties, conduct disorders or communication problems. Ensure there is a referral process for any problems to be indentified early.	
	Developing independence continues as well as developing self-esteem – may be pushing boundaries; moral and spiritual development	Reward positive behaviour and where possible ignore the bad (biting should not be tolerated)	
	Developing empathy and respect for others	Awareness of 'sameness' and 'differences' – consider other cultures and religions, etc.	

Age		
3–4 years	Learning to read and write	Books, writing materials, interactions with adults, include quiet times, etc.
	Cognitive development – learning about world outside	Looking at nature; walks and trips out of the setting
	Control of bladder and bowels (toilet training); daytime control common before night-time control	Some children will find toileting very difficult, particularly when not at home. Good communication with parents vital.
4–5 years	Continuing cognitive development – understanding of more complex concepts	Preparation for school: increasingly diverse materials for children to explore; be aware of varying levels of ability
	Improving balance and spatial awareness, Walking heel to toe, standing on one leg, hopping, skipping, control of bladder at night	Neurological difficulties such as dyspraxia may be noticed

and develop (HGI, 2010). This separates human beings from animals and where these needs are met effectively, individuals will be free from mental health problems and will be able to contribute to society and ultimately, the continuation of the species (HGI, 2010).

In the first instance, an individual needs air, water, food, safety, shelter, privacy, warmth and sleep (Maslow, 1972). In addition, our emotional needs include: the need to give and receive attention (attachment); to have a sense of control (autonomy); to have at least one other person who accepts us unconditionally; to feel part of a wider community (socialisation); to have a sense of meaning or purpose to our lives and to be respected (have status) (HGI, 2010). These can be considered within the Early Years settings as a base or guideline for the resources necessary to provide children with these basic human needs.

Learning and development

Human beings are unique in their ability to learn and remember information; to recognise concepts and the relationship between them; and to apply learned information to their behaviour in an adaptive way (problem solving) (Gross, 2005). Five areas of development are often identified within child developmental theory and are explicit with the EYFS (DCSF, 2008). This section will discuss these five areas of development: physical, intellectual, language, emotional and social (PILES). The relationship of these areas of development to supporting learning in the Early Years setting will also be outlined.

The Early Years Foundation Stage Learning Goals

Personal, Social and Emotional Development

Communication, Language and Literacy

Problem Solving, Reasoning and Numeracy

Knowledge and Understanding of the World

Physical Development

Creative Development

Physical development

The physical development of the brain has been discussed previously in this chapter in relation to social and emotional development.

The brain and the spinal cord form the central nervous system (CNS), which receives and interprets stimuli and sends messages to parts of the body such as the muscles and glands (Neill and Knowles, 2004). The CNS is crucial in the development of the control of movement and co-ordination (Neill and Knowles, 2004) and it is also important in terms of cognitive development. Without the physical structures within the CNS (the neurons and synapses), the electrical impulses which are translated into thought processes would be impossible (Neill and Knowles, 2004). The development of the CNS begins very early in foetal development (from the first two weeks following conception) and physical damage to the brain may impact on all areas of development and learning (Chamley et al., 2007). Damage to the brain can occur at any stage of development from foetal development in the uterus through to adulthood and is caused by different factors such as trauma and infection (Chamley et al., 2005). The location of the damaged area is significant to what part of development is affected.

Table 5.2 gives an overview of the physical milestones that children are expected to reach at different ages and factors that may affect this; this must be taken in context as children will develop at very different rates and times. However, it is important to have an awareness of these milestones in order to identify any problems early that may need the support of other agencies (DCSF, 2008).

The control we have over physical development varies, but growth in children is seen as an important indicator of a child's health and well-being (DH, 2009). A balanced diet is very important for the growth of muscles and bones and brain development (Chamley et al., 2007). The energy needed for growth, movement and thinking processes is provided by the food we eat and in terms of child development there are two particularly important times for growth: the first two years of life and during puberty. The recommendation for weaning babies is from around six months (Food Standards Agency [FSA], 2010a). The balance of good health means ensuring that children have a balance of the major food groups; around a third of the intake should be fruit and vegetables (5 or more portions per day), around a third of the intake should be starchy foods (carbohydrates) (5 or more portions). The rest of the diet is made up of: protein (2 portions); dairy products (2–3 portions); and fats and sugars should make up only a very small part of the daily intake, particularly for children (FSA, 2010b). There have been recent suggestions that fish oils help to increase the concentration levels of children (Child of Our Time, 2008); the FSA advises that there has not been enough supporting evidence for this suggestion yet. It is generally considered more beneficial to eat oily fish twice a week rather than taking capsules, but this must be done with some caution due to the possibility of pollutants such as mercury in fish (FSA, 2010b). Further advice and information can be obtain via the Food Standards Agency website (FSA, 2010b).

Equally, physical exercise is also important for normal growth; there has been recent evidence to suggest that children live very sedentary lives for a variety of reasons (Change for Life, 2010). The growth of computers and television in our lives has appeared to have a detrimental effect on physical activity levels and obesity problems for all of us, but in particular, for young children (DCSF, 2009). Parental fear is also a factor in allowing children some freedom to explore the outdoors. This, coupled with a perceived lack of safe, open spaces, impacts on physical development (Healthy Schools, 2010). Interestingly, recent statistics suggest that violent child deaths have significantly fallen by 40 per cent since the 1970s (*Guardian*, 2010). Children have a natural curiosity to explore and experiment with new experiences and Early Years settings can have a positive effect on this by providing safe areas for exploration and opportunities to practise both gross and fine motor skills.

The National Healthy Schools Programme (NHSP) was introduced in 1999 to encourage settings to promote healthy behaviours among children, young people, parents and also adults

Table 5.2: Physical development: a summary

AGE	EXPECTED PHYSICAL ABILITY	FACTORS AFFECTING DEVELOPMENT
0–3 months	Growth	Poor nutrition, neglect, poverty/metabolic disorders
	Reflex actions: grasping, feeding, sucking, stepping or walking, kicking	Birth trauma/brain damage/cerebral palsy/infection, e.g. meningitis
	With experience/stimulation: following movements visually, smiling	Poor feeding will affect growth
	Follows sounds with head	Cleft palate/hair lip
		Gastric reflux
	Babies can be born with teeth!	Pyloric stenosis (narrowing of the muscles at the top of the stomach causing vomiting)
		Genetic abnormalities such as Down Syndrome/cystic fibrosis/fragile X
		Hearing problems
3–6 months	Growth	Injury/brain damage/cerebral palsy
	Independent head holding: size of the head grows along with brain growth	
	Holding objects; hand–eye co-ordination improves, rolling over	Neglect, lack of practice with fine motor skills
	Laughing, smiling, making sounds; muscles for these skills developing	Lack of stimulation or adult interaction

	Tooth development	Poor diet or feeding
6 months– 1 year	Weaning on to solid food	Poor diet
	Sitting, crawling, improving fine motor skills and hand–eye co-ordination	Nutritional disorders/fussy eating/bowel disorders such as coeliac disease
	Making eye contact, interacting, laughing, developing language	Communication difficulties such autism may become noticeable
	Tooth development	
1–2 years	Standing, walking, balance, improving fine and gross motor skills: self-feeding	Neurological conditions such as muscular dystrophy
2–3 years	More confident walking, running, spatial awareness, two feet jumping	Accidents common at this age
	Language development – development of teeth may affect this (lisp)	
3–4 years	Control of bladder and bowels (toilet training): daytime control common before night-time control	Physical problems with urinary tract or bowel
		Endocrine problems (pituitary gland)
4–5 years	Improving balance and spatial awareness, Walking heel to toe, standing on one leg, hopping, skipping, control of bladder at night	Neurological difficulties such as dyspraxia may be noticed

working within those settings. In particular, the focus has been on improving the health and well-being of children and young people to improve educational achievement, encourage inclusion and improve inter-agency working (NHSP, 2010). This initiative is extending out into the Early Years settings and is in line with the EYFS principles (DCSF, 2008). It will enable practitioners to demonstrate how they are able to achieve two of the outcomes from *Every Child Matters*: 'being healthy' and 'staying safe' (DH/DfES, 2004). It is also in line with the Government strategy for children and young people's health outlined in *Healthy Lives, Brighter Futures* (DCSF/DH, 2009).

So, the physical development of children can be an indicator of their overall health and well-being. This impacts on the other four areas of child development which are commonly identified, and explored below.

Intellectual development (cognition)

> *Tell me and I will forget, show me and I may remember, involve me and I will understand*
>
> (Chinese proverb)

There are different theories as to how we, as human beings, learn but there is general agreement that learning involves a relatively permanent change and that it is dependent upon past experiences. How the change occurs and what processes cause the change is debated by psychologists (Gross, 2005). Cognitive learning describes the way in which the human mind processes information to develop an understanding of the world and adapt to the environment (Gross, 2005). This will depend upon a number of physical and psychological factors including: the amount of external stimulation; the growth of CNS; memory; motivation; and intelligence. The ability to constantly change and adapt information in order to progress or learn is the key to human survival. Piaget is perhaps the most well-known psychologist who discussed cognitive development in terms of 'schemas', which may be described as building blocks of intelligent behaviour (Gross, 2005). These schemas are ways of understanding the complex world around us and adapting what we know already to different experiences and situations. Piaget described three fundamental processes which are common throughout these schemas: assimilation; accommodation; and equilibrium (Gross, 2005). So, when faced with a new situation, we try to use any knowledge that we already have to understand it (assimilation), if what we know is not enough to explain the experience, we must accommodate this new information to adapt our pre-existing knowledge. Once this is achieved, we can be in a 'balanced' state (equilibrium) until another new situation is faced. As individuals develop, they will have greater experiences to draw upon when faced with different situations and this helps to maintain the equilibrium for longer. Memory is an important aspect of this process; without the ability to remember the information in the first place, a permanent change will not be possible.

Motivation will also play a part in how we learn and is key to working in Early Years settings. Motivation drives us forwards, makes us curious and enables us to explore, experiment and take risks in order to learn (Bruce, 2010). External factors may interrupt motivation – for example, a lack of encouragement, instilling feelings of guilt, a shortage of appropriate stimulus or neglect (Howarth, 2007). Internal factors will also affect motivation such as personality, self-confidence or self-esteem.

ACTIVITY

Think about what has motivated you to learn in the past. What were the key things that drove you forward and can you categorise them into either intrinsic factors (internal influences such as personality, self-determination, etc.) or extrinsic factors (external influences such as the environment, family expectations or peer pressure).

Intelligence

Intelligence is a difficult concept for which everyone has their own particular theory or idea. Perhaps intelligence could be described as the ability to perform particular cognitive tasks, but is this about having a good memory to regurgitate information, an ability to articulate ideas, possessing good interpersonal skills, or is it more about being able to solve a problem (Sternberg, 2000)? Sternberg (2000) describes both lay people's interpretation of intelligence and also what the 'experts' say. There seems little consensus overall but there are some common themes involving the ability to learn and adapt to different situations and the use of 'higher thinking', such as reasoning, problem solving and decision making. These are evident in the EYFS in the form of: Problem Solving, Reasoning and Numeracy.

ACTIVITY

Find out about Howard Gardner's theory of multiple intelligences and observe the children in your setting. Can you identify any of the intelligences that he describes?

Certainly, in the UK today, measurements of children's ability in these areas are used to 'judge' what learning has occurred in the form of Standard Assessment Tests (SATs) and this is measured against children of the same age. Early Years practitioners may feel under pressure from both parents and professional bodies such as Ofsted in terms of 'academic' results but the individuality of each child must be respected. This will mean recognising that children will have different learning styles and there are many theories (and tests) around these learning differences. The basic differences are between those who learn predominantly visually (observing, reading and writing), aurally and orally (by listening and talking) or kinaesthetically (touch and movement) (Bruce, 2010). These styles should be recognised with some caution as although a child may have a preference for one or the other, often there is a mixture of styles in different settings and circumstances. However, an awareness of the individual styles of the children in the setting may be useful, as well as a self-awareness by the practitioners of their own learning style (Bruce, 2010). Providing a variety of activities that stimulate children in different ways and allowing children some freedom of choice in how they learn is a useful way of treating each child as unique and encouraging independence.

Language and communication

Learning to communicate begins at a very early age and children learn quickly, given the right circumstances, to get what they need. To have their basic needs met, they learn to get attention by crying; babies have a particularly loud cry in relation to their size (Livingstone, 2008). Babies are born with some ability to read the main emotions such as happiness and sadness in adult faces and they also have the ability to express these feelings themselves (Livingstone, 2008).

They learn to recognise the cues of adults as they learn to 'please', e.g. a child learns that they can make an adult laugh with a particular action and will repeat that action to get a response. As social animals, human beings crave attention from others and, ideally, the innate desire is to have positive attention. However, children with particular communication difficulties, or children who are experiencing neglect or other forms of abuse, may display negative behaviour in order to communicate their anxieties or frustrations (Herbert, 2005). Equally, children may communicate in other ways their emotional or physical difficulties such as becoming withdrawn or mute when their emotional or social needs are not being met (Horwath, 2007).

Babies begin to use noises early on in development and start to experiment with their own voices, starting with cooing, gurgling and laughing sounds (Livingstone, 2007). The development of language is debated in the literature; is language a natural development or is it learned? Chomsky (cited in Bruce, 2010) argued that children possess a built-in system called a language acquisition device, which allows the brain to develop language and that there is a critical period for this. He argued that after puberty it becomes much more difficult to learn a language that one has not been exposed to regularly. He suggested that cognitive ability was not necessarily a factor in developing language as most children will learn to speak.

However, social learning theorists such as Vygotsky argued that language was developed through interaction with others (Bruce, 2010). Vygotsky (cited in Bruce, 2010) discussed the role that adults (and others) play in interacting with children through a *zone of proximal development*. This describes the distance between what the child knows and the potential learning that may occur given the right circumstances with interaction with others. What the child brings to a learning situation may be some natural ability (their actual level of development) and what others may bring (the potential level of development). Through interacting with those with more experience, learning occurs through a process and language develops.

There is some evidence to support both these theories, particularly as children do show a natural desire to communicate, but the environment seems to play an equally important role in the development of speech and language skills.

> **ACTIVITY**
> Consider the evidence for these two theories for yourself in your setting. Can you draw any conclusions from practice? What is your experience of children learning language and communication? How do you support and encourage language development?

Emotional and social development

Over time, attitudes towards children have changed dramatically; children have become a focal point of attention in today's society by both their parents and the 'state' (Jones, 2009; BBC, 2010a). On the one hand, they are seen as vulnerable and dependent and in need of protection (BBC, 2010b). The introduction of the ISA is evidence of the view that society needs to protect vulnerable children from significant harm. This organisation is set up to monitor all individuals who work regularly with children and is an extension of the CRB check (ISA, 2010). However, we also have another view of children as antisocial and being out of the control of their parents

(Jones, 2009; Cameron, 2010). Children may be demonised by adults and, in some cases, feared, and this creates an environment of mistrust (Layard and Dunn, 2009).

The socialisation process describes the way in which children learn the rules, norms and values of society, and what behaviour is expected of them as they grow up (Marsh and Keating, 2006). It is considered important that children develop into 'citizens' who are able to 'make a contribution' and 'achieve economic well-being'; these are explicit within the five outcomes from ECM (DH/DfES, 2004). The development of the concept of citizenship is reflected within the work done around building social capital. Social capital is about encouraging communities to work together to improve the lives of all those living and working in that local area by building social networks (Respect, 2010), and one could argue that Early Years practitioners may be at the heart of this as they work with families and the future citizens.

Society has rules and expectations of its members and a healthy, 'compliant' population may be seen to be the most productive in terms of economic stability and the continuation of our culture in the broadest sense (Herbert, 2003). This, of course, is highly debatable in ethical terms and many sociologists would argue that society discourages individuality and excludes those who are marginalised or 'different' (Marsh and Keating, 2006). For example, those who have complex health or social needs; the disabled; the mentally ill; those with learning difficulties; or those who choose to live in a different way such as travelling families. Understanding and valuing diversity is a key theme running through many government policy documents and is explicit in the EYFS (DCSF, 2008). Therefore, treating children as unique individuals with specific developmental needs according to their abilities and level of competence, is key in Early Years settings (DCSF, 2008).

The Early Years setting provides an opportunity to develop young people in the skills they need to 'fit in' to society as a whole and become independent. It is also in a position to identify children who behave differently or who find it difficult to learn the 'social rules' and become socially competent. Generally, children learn the social rules initially from their parents or carers. The family's moral and spiritual values and beliefs are passed on to children and this will vary from family to family depending on influences such as the environment, family structures, culture and religion. Children will then be exposed to the outside world with perhaps a conflicting set of rules and this can create difficulties.

The 'social tasks' of children begin as babies as they learn to communicate their needs. Attachment to others enables them to have both their physical and emotional needs met – food, security, attention and love (Gerhardt, 2004; HGI, 2010). As they grow, children develop physical skills such as eating independently, control of the bladder and bowel, speech and language. They also learn to adapt their behaviour to continue to have their needs met – for example, learning to share, to please adults and peers, learning right from wrong and to have self-control. These skills may be described in terms of learning by observing others and by trial and error (Bruce, 2010). Children who are observing aggressive behaviour in the home may copy that behaviour in the EY setting; if children are rewarded for their behaviour, they are more likely to repeat it. The reward may not necessarily be a tangible one; it may simply be attention. Many parenting programmes are based on these theories to help parents to understand their child's behaviour and make changes to how they approach discipline. Specifically, that positive behaviour should be rewarded and negative behaviour ignored where possible; the positive behaviour will then increase and the negative behaviour will decrease. This is a very simplistic view and there may be many factors which will affect the results, but it forms a reasonable basis for parenting techniques and is underpinned by some theory (Bandura and Skinner, cited in Gross, 2005).

The ability of children to adapt their behaviour will also depend on their level of cognitive ability, their age, or if they have a specific behavioural problem. For example, children with learning difficulties, conduct disorders, communication difficulties or psychiatric problems will need to be assessed according to individual need and managed appropriately. Settings need a specific behaviour policy that is available to parents and an awareness of the referral processes for children with special educational needs. This can be found within the *Special Educational Needs: Code of Practice* (DfES, 2001).

CHAPTER SUMMARY

- This chapter has explored the four themes within the EYFS.
- The role of the key worker has been emphasised as it aims to ensure that children develop positive relationships that support their emotional development. Providing a range of activities will cater for different levels of cognitive ability and also different learning styles.
- The importance and benefits of Foundation Degrees in providing the training and education to contribute to the CPD of the Early Years workforce has been explored.

Chapter 6 takes a wider approach to Early Years, looking at some current debates that concern all those working in the childcare sector, whether in care or education. It also takes an international approach looking to see what is going on in the rest of Europe, New Zealand and Australia that we might learn from. It looks at the development of education in the UK and at recent reports that are having an effect on the way our children are taught. The importance of inclusion is the final theme.

REFERENCES

BBC (2010a) *The British Family*. BBC2 productions, broadcast on 1 February 2010.
BBC (2010b) *Panorama* BBC1 productions, broadcast on 8 February 2010.
BBC (2008) *Child of Our Time* (2008) BBC productions: broadcast 5 June, BBC, Open University.
Brookes, L (2006) *The Story of Childhood*. London: Bloomsbury Publishing.
Bruce, T (2010) *Early Childhood: A Guide For Students*. London: Sage.
Cameron, D (2010). *Broken Britain, can we fix it?* Available online from: www.telegraph.co.uk/family/5805205/Broken-Britain---can-we-fix-it.html (accessed 30 January 2010).
Child Growth Foundation (2010) Available online on: http://www.childgrowthfoundation.org/ (accessed 30 January 2010).
Chinese proverb (2010) Available online from: www.quotationspage.com/quote/4462.html (accessed 7 February 2010).
Chamley, CA, Carson, P, Randall, D and Sandwell, M (2007) *Developmental Anatomy and Physiology of Children: A Practical Approach*. London: Elsevier.
DCSF (2004) *Early Support; Helping Every Child Succeed. Information for Parent: Deafness*. Nottingham: DCSF.
DCSF (2007a) *The Children's Plan*. Nottingham: DCSF.
DCSF (2007b) *Every Parent Matters*. Nottingham: DCSF.

DCSF (2008) *Statutory Framework for the Early Years Foundation Stage: Setting the Standard for Learning, development and care for children from birth to five.* Nottingham: DCSF.

DCSF/DH (2009) *Healthy Lives, Brighter Futures; the strategy for children and young people's health.* London: DCSF/DH.

DoH/DfES (2004) *Every Child Matters: Change for Children.* London: DH/DfES.

Department of Health (DoH) (2009) *The Child Health Promotion Programme.* London: DoH.

Food Standards Agency (2010a) *Weaning your baby.* Available online from: www.eatwell.gov.uk/agesandstages/baby/weaning/ (accessed 20 January 2010).

Food Standards Agency (2010b) *Ages and Stages.* Available online from: www.eatwell.gov.uk/asksam/agesandstages/childrenandbabies/ (accessed 20 January 2010).

Gerhardt, S (2004) *Why Love Matters: How Affection Shapes a Baby's Brain.* Hove: Brunner-Routledge.

Gross, R (2005) *The Science of Mind and Behaviour.* London: Hodder Arnold.

Guardian (2010) *Violent Deaths of children down 40%* Available online from: www.guardian.co.uk/society/2010/feb/04/fewer-violent-child-deaths (accessed 7 February 2010).

Hall, D and Elliman D (2007) *Health For All Children.* Oxford: Oxford University Press.

Herbert, M (2003) *Typical and Atypical Child Development.* Oxford: Blackwell Publishing.

Herbert M (2005) *Developmental Problems of Childhood and Adolescence.* Oxford. Blackwell Publishing.

Horwath, J (2007) *Child Neglect.* Basingstoke: Palgrave Macmillan.

HM Government (2004) *The Children Act.* London: HM Government.

ISA (2010) *The Independent Safeguarding Authority.* Available online from: www.isa-gov.org.uk/ (accessed 8 February 2010).

Jones, P (2009) *Rethinking Childhood: Attitudes in Contemporary Society.* London: Continuum Books.

Layard, R and Dunn, J (2000) *A Good Childhood.* London: The Children's Society.

Lindon, J (2007) *Understanding Child Development.* London: Hodder Arnold.

Livingstone, T (2005) *Child of Our Time: Early Learning.* London: Bantam Press.

Livingstone, T (2008) *Child of Our Time: Early Learning.* London: Bantam Press.

Marsh, I and Keating, M (2006) (Editors) *Sociology: Making Sense of Society.* 3rd edition. Harlow: Pearson Education.

Martin, GN, Carlson, NR and Buskist, W (2007) *Psychology.* 3rd edition. Harlow: Pearson Education.

Maslow, A (1972) *The Farther Reaches of Human Nature.* New York: The Viking Press, cited in Gross, R (1991) *Psychology: The Science of Mind and Behaviour.* London: Hodder & Stoughton.

Morris, S (2009) Vanessa George Jailed for Sex Abuse. Available online from: www.guardian.co.uk/uk/2009/dec/15/vanessa-george-jailed-child-sex-abuse (accessed 5 January 2010).

NHS *Change for Life* (2010) Available online from: www.nhs.uk/Change4Life (accessed 13 January 2010).

NHSP (2010) *Promoting health Early Years settings* Available online from: http://www.teaching expertise.com/articles/promoting-healthy-early-years-settings-3183 (accessed 9 February 2010).

National Healthy Schools Programme (2010) Available online from: http://home.healthyschools.gov.uk/ (accessed on 1 February 2010).

National Statistics Online (2010) Divorces: England and Wales. Available online from: www.statistics.gov.uk/cci/nugget.asp?id=170 (accessed 12 Janauary 2010).

Neill, S and Knowles, H (2004) *The Biology of Child Health.* Basingstoke: Palgrave Macmillan.

Newman, BM and Newman, PR (2009) *Development through Life – A Psychosocial Approach.* 10th edition. USA: Wadsworth Cengage Learning.

Norton, P and Norfolk, A (2010) Sadistic Edlington boy torturers jailed for at least five years. *The Times*.

Protective Behaviours (2010) *Protective Behaviours: UK* Available online from: www.protectivebehaviours.co.uk/ (accessed 13 January 2010).

Schaffer, HR (2004) *Introducing Child Psychology*. Oxford: Blackwell Publishing.

Socrates available online from: www.s9.com/Biography/Socrates (accessed 30 January 2010).

Sternberg, RJ (2000) *Handbook of Intelligence*. Cambridge: Cambridge University Press.

Respect (2010) *Strengthening Communities* Available online from: www.asb.homeoffice.gov.uk/article.aspx?id=9070 (accessed 9 February 2010).

The Humans Givens Institute (2010) *The Human Givens Approach*. Available online from: www.hgi.org.uk/archive/human-givens.htm (accessed 18 January 2010).

UNICEF (2007) *Child Poverty in Perspective: An overview of Child Well-being in Rich Countries*. Florence: UNICEF Innocenti Research Centre.

World Health Organization (WHO) (2002) *World Report on Violence and Health*. Geneva, WHO.

6 CURRENT DEBATES IN EARLY YEARS EDUCATION AND PROVISION

CHAPTER OBJECTIVES

By the end of this chapter you will:

- be able to participate in a range of current debates within Early Years care and education;
- appreciate some of the international perspectives in Early Years provision;
- understand staff gender issues in Early Years;
- be able to analyse the philosophy of inclusion within your own and other settings.

Introduction

This chapter explains to the reader how specific knowledge of certain issues can help them with their wider knowledge and skills. It explores international perspectives in Early Years education and discusses staff gender issues in the Early Years. The issue of inclusive Early Years provision is debated before looking at the changing position of the child in the centre of this field as the rights of the child continue to be debated.

Debates within Early Years practice

When working in your settings, do you often feel that you do not know what is happening in the outside world? You become immersed in the very busy everyday life of the setting and the changing needs of the children, parents, staff and other professionals. Do you find time to read current textbooks, newspapers, Early Years journals or to look at relevant websites? The organisations and government departments listed below are useful sources of information.

- The Children's Workforce, Development Council (CWDC);
- The Department for Children, Schools and Families (DCSF);
- The National Children's Bureau (NCB);
- Open Eye.

You will probably all relate to this experience to some extent and answer, 'No'.

However, the importance of reading and keeping up to date with current issues and debates surrounding Early Years practice cannot be overemphasised. Reading headlines in the newspapers and journals can promote thought and reflection on situations and practice within the settings in which you work. Reflection with your teams should then promote debate, which in turn should support changes in practice to enhance the provision for the children, parents and team, as discussed in Chapters 1 and 4.

The range of debates involving Early Years theory, legislation and practice is enormous and for some very emotive. Many debates have been on-going for several years, for example the age that children commence reading and writing, and the statutory school age for entry into compulsory schooling.

Listed below is a range of debates affecting provision in Early Years settings:

- Early Years Foundation Stage Framework
  - learning through play;
  - the use of ICT in Early Years settings;
  - indoor and outdoor play;
  - children taking risks such as climbing trees;
  - Open Eye, linked to the learning outcomes for Communication, Language and Literacy.
- Statutory age for starting school.
- One-point entry to school each September for 4 year olds.
- International approaches to EY and statutory school ages.
- International approaches to reading and writing.
- Early Years Foundation Funding Status – free sessions for 3–4 year olds, possibly for 2–3 year olds.
- Poverty – ending.
- Sure Start – Children's Centres, are they achieving their targets?
- Extended hours.
- Shared care.
- Paying grandparents.
- Inclusion.
- Responding to the learning needs of boys.
- The rights of the child.
- The target of the CWDC to have a graduate in every setting by 2015.
- Pay linked to improved qualifications.
- Early Years Professional Status (EYPS)
  - EYPS → Parity with Qualified Teacher Status
- Staff gender Issues.
- Bureaucracy.
- Self-assessment forms.
- Ofsted Inspections – changes.

ACTIVITY

How will knowledge of the above debates help to enhance your knowledge and understanding of childcare provision, children's development and learning, working with parents and in multi-professional teams?

Think about this question, reflect on the paragraph above and in groups discuss your thoughts. Identify one area/issue within your setting that could be improved if your knowledge and understanding of national debates was deeper.

In many respects the question is linked to Chapter 4 where you explored the journey to and the results of becoming an EYP. For the most part, it was about extending your knowledge and understanding of all aspects of childcare that are required of an Early Years professional in order to ensure the quality of experiences for the children who attend your settings. This was achieved through reflective practice, linking your reflections to the individual needs of the children and their parents, and using your extended knowledge and understanding of child development and theories of child development. However, as already stated above, debate results in reflection upon your own practice, sharing ideas, using ideas to respond to situations that have been causing concerns and 'problem solving'.

In order to be able to respond appropriately to children and their parents, it is essential to be able to speak to them about different types of provision, to be able to explain why you work in the way that you do, to have a full understanding of the styles of children's learning and development; in other words, to be able to answer any questions they may ask. The first principle of the EYFS, as you all know, is the 'Unique Child'. What does unique child mean? A child would respond that it means there is only one child like me with my individual care and learning needs to which you, with my parents, are required to respond. Deepening and extending your own knowledge and understanding across all aspects of Early Years learning and development, including international perspectives, will ease the demands of working in the sector. Learning about international issues relating to Early Years does not mean you have to agree, but extension of knowledge results in enabling you to present an informed, balanced and reasoned debate.

The debates chosen to be explored in more detail are as follows.

International perspectives on Early Years provision
- Communication, language and literacy.
- Statutory school age.
- The philosophies of Steiner and Montessori, including debate about their delivery of the EYFS, communication, language and literacy.
- Graduates in Early Years settings.

Inclusive Early Years provision
- The requirements of the EYFS.
- Ensuring that everyone connected with the setting feels included.
- The rights of the child.

Staffing issues
- Gender issues when staffing Early Years settings.

These topics have been chosen because they are prominent as national debates and may have direct influence to everyday practice in your settings, whether working in day care, preschool, nursery school or schools. However, it is hoped that while researching for your assignments the other debates listed above, or new debates that may arise, are used to support statements made or to create discussion. While exploring international approaches it must be appreciated that, as identified by Moss et al. (1999) and Rinaldi (1999) there are many cultural, political and historical perspectives and choices that may influence the provision for children.

There has been much emotive debate online, in the press and through recent research about the EYFS and the approach to Communication, Language and Literacy, particularly the requirements of the Early Learning Goals (ELGs) linked to this area of learning. Questions have been asked about when children should start compulsory school. The UK has one of the youngest ages for starting school. In many instances, children now start in Reception at the age of just four years, having had their birthday in August, although this is not compulsory. The compulsory age to start school in the UK is five years of age, but many parents have concerns about being able to send their child/children to the school of their choice or within their catchment area if they do not send them to the Reception class at the age of four. In Europe and many other countries, the starting age for compulsory, full-time schooling is six or seven years of age (see Table 6.1 below). Learning through play is valued and children do not start reading and writing until they commence statutory schooling.

Table 6.1: A range of international statutory school ages

COUNTRY	STATUTORY SCHOOL AGE	COMMENTS
Australia	6	But can be earlier, e.g. Queensland if permission granted by regional General Manager for Schools.
Bavaria	6	1 August for those 6 years old by 30 June in same year.
Bulgaria	7	See paragraph on Eastern European provision on page 94.
Canada	6	Those who are 6 by 1 September. However, this varies from state to state, e.g. British Colombia and Saskatchewan children must be in school by their seventh birthday.
Croatia	7	See paragraph on Eastern European provision on page 94.
Czech Republic	7	See paragraph on Eastern European provision on page 94.
Denmark	6	Nursery education is statutory from the age of 3 years.
England	5	However, many children are commencing Reception classes at the age of 4 years.
France	6	September of year when 6 years.
Germany	6	
Hungary	7	See paragraph on Eastern European provision on page 94.

Table 6.1: Continued

COUNTRY	STATUTORY SCHOOL AGE	COMMENTS
N. Ireland	4	This is the youngest age for the start of compulsory schooling.
Italy	6	Children are not actively taught to read and write but many are able to by the time they start compulsory schooling (Hirst, 2001).
Macedonia	7	See paragraph on Eastern European provision on page 94.
New Zealand	5	Similar to UK.
Portugal	6	Similar to Spain.
Romania	7	See paragraph on Eastern European provision on page 94.
Serbia	7	See paragraph on Eastern European provision on page 94.
Scotland	5	In line with England.
Slovakia	7	See paragraph on Eastern European provision on page 94.
Spain	6	Preschool 3–6 years, not compulsory but government provides a free place if requested.
Sweden	6	
Wales	5	In line with England, but the emphasis on play-based learning has been in place for a longer period of time.

ACTIVITY

Discuss this table in small groups.

What are your immediate thoughts and what is your opinion about the statutory school age?

What would you recommend for your setting and for schools?

International perspectives on Early Years provision

The main focus of the debate presented here is communication, language and literacy that links very closely to the debate about the commencement of statutory schooling in Europe and the UK. Three comparative approaches to Early Years care and education will also be considered. However, before embarking on the debates, it is worth reflecting briefly on the history of Early Years in the UK, as illustrated in Chapter 2, and the comments of Hawkins

(1998) that the development of Early Years provision has internationally followed the teachings of Rousseau, Froebel, Montessori and Dewey who advocated the need for young children to learn through play. The development of Early Years provision has progressed irregularly and in many instances regressed because the needs of the sector have been neglected, as in the USA, and influenced by *political ideologues who have suppressed or ignored these forward steps* in England (Hawkins, 1998).

The three comparative approaches to Early Years education to be considered in preparation for future debate are:

- Italy – Reggio Emilia;
- New Zealand – Te Whariki;
- UK – EYFS – England.

Italy

The Italian approach to Early Years education has been considered by many international Early Years Professionals, for example those in the USA, including Lally (2001) who hoped that the trend for the curriculum in the USA to become very prescriptive, would be reversed. In the UK, Abbott and Nutbrown (2001) have written about the Reggio Emilia approach and have been inspired by the passion and vision of Italian pedagogues. Compare the two quotes below. The first quote, according to Lally (2001), is the general Italian philosophy:

> *That children's motivation toward mastery, self-regulation, and social commerce and their reliance on relationships with trusted caregivers for support and guidance must be central to program planning.*
>
> (Lally in Gandini and Edwards, 2001, p20)

Although Lally states this as Italian philosophy, compare this to the following where Malaguzzi expresses the Reggio Emilia approach as:

> *our image of the child is rich in potential, strong, powerful, competent and most of all connected to adults and children.*
>
> (Malaguzzi (1997) in Abbott and Nutbrown, 2001, p5)

These two comparative philosophies convey a similar approach.

In order to meet the individual needs of the children, staff in Italy, cited by Lally in Gandini and Edwards (2001), are trained to search for children's natural interests and curiosity. Consider the approach used by Reggio Emilia in Italy. All members of staff have a commitment to ensure a deep understanding of the children through listening to them, observing them, ensuring there is time to discuss them and to work co-operatively within their entire team and with the parents. Abbott and Nutbrown (2001) report on a visit to Reggio Emilia in 1999 when the director of Reggio preschools asked the following questions.

- What do we hope for children?
- What do we expect from children?
- What is the relationship between school and research?
- What is the relationship between school and education?

- What is the relationship between school, family and society?
- What is the relationship between school and life?
- Is school a preparation for, or part of, life?

(Abbott and Nutbrown, 2001, p6)

ACTIVITY

Think about the following questions and statements.

Do we consider our own practice in this way? The word 'school' is substituted by 'Early Years'.

- Do we consider the relationships between Early Years and research, education, family and society?
- Do you think that the Early Years is a preparation for, or part of, life?
- Is high-quality education for the Early Years the responsibility of all adult citizens?

Abbott and Nutbrown (2001) also reflected on the international challenge posed by Spaggiari (1996) to provide high-quality educational services for young children, stating that *it can be seen as the responsibility of all adult citizens.*

How do these questions and the last statement by Spaggiari reflect the four principles of the EYFS, the five outcomes of ECM and the target of the CWDC to employ a graduate, with EYPS, in every setting by 2015?

Italian children usually attend preschools until they are six years of age. Hirst (2001, in Abbott and Nutbrown, 2001) speaks about the fact that children are not actively taught to read and write. However, resources are available to facilitate mark making and discussion, and to support the child's desire to read, write and communicate, resulting in many children reading and writing before attending school. Therefore, the staff are following the lead of the child by providing opportunities in response to desire.

New Zealand

Te Whariki – New Zealand Early Childhood curriculum

Nuttal (2003) speaks about early childhood education as being a distinctive cultural form in its own right and, prior to the introduction of an early childhood curriculum about the anxieties that existed within the workforce about the introduction of a specific curriculum for the Early Years. Te Whariki was introduced in 1993 (Nuttal, 2003), not without some reservations, and became statutory in 2002.

The Te Whariki curriculum was developed and is delivered to all Early Years children in New Zealand to meet the needs of the diverse bicultural country with dominant Western curriculum ideologies to ensure inclusion of the voice of the Maori natives. However, as described by Ritchie (2003), some regions of New Zealand were not demonstrating full commitment to this bicultural development. To include two cultures and for Early Years settings to be fully committed to the bicultural curriculum sounds relatively straightforward, but as Ritchie moves on to point out, *cultures are constantly changing and shifting*.

Te Whariki is the Maori word for 'woven mat' and is spoken of as weaving the curriculum.

The principles of learning and development are described as a framework of:

- *Whakamana – Empowerment;*
- *Kotahitanga – Holistic development;*
- *Whānau Tangata – Family and Community;*
- *ngā Honotanga – Relationships.*

(New Zealand Ministry of Education website, accessed 9 February 2010)

The following are the strands and goals listed by Fleer (2003) that arise from the above principles. However, Fleer goes on to say that the two languages do not translate exactly.

Maori	Western
• *Mana atua*	*Well-being*
• *Mana whenua*	*Belonging*
• *Mana tangata*	*Contribution*
• *Mana reo*	*Communication*
• *Mana aoturoa*	*Exploration*

(Fleer, 2003, in Nuttal, 2003, p250)

David et al. in Pugh and Duffey (2010) state that:

One of the central claims of both Te Whariki and the New Zealand 10-Year Strategic Plan for Early Childhood is that they are research and sector informed.

(David et al., in Pugh and Duffey, 2010, p41)

They also speak about children learning in communities of practice and in the care of informed professionals. Again, this connects with the target of the CWDC to have an EYP, that is, a professional who is well informed about the needs of Early Years children and their families in every setting by 2015.

The age for children commencing statutory schooling in New Zealand is their fifth birthday. This is when formal teaching for reading and writing commences, in line with the UK, apart from Northern Ireland, which commences compulsory schooling at the age of four years. Recent research in New Zealand by Dr Sebastian Suggate, conducted over a three-year period and involving 400 children who had been taught to read at five years in comparison with children who had attended Steiner Schools where reading and writing is taught at a later age, found that by the age of eleven years there was no difference in the reading abilities of the children. He also found that most children who had difficulties with reading at a younger age had caught up by the age of eight to nine years (www.literacytrust.org.uk/literacynews/earlyyears.html, accessed 9 February 2010).

In New Zealand, transition to compulsory schooling, known as years 1–6, from Early Years education is supported by a school that:

- fosters a child's relationships with teachers and other children and affirms their identity;
- builds on the learning experiences that the child brings with them;
- considers the child's whole experience of school;
- is welcoming of family and whānau.

This approach builds upon the children's previous learning by making connections with their earlier experiences. There is a strong focus on literacy and numeracy and the development of values and key competencies across all learning areas.

The following quote was read in a paper written by Pakai:

HE WHAKATAUKI

HE KOHANGA PIPI I TE PAPA

KA AITUA

HE KOHANGA PIPI IKEIKE I TE PARI

KA RERE I TE AO

Translation: Baby birds nesting on the ground are subject to misfortune (danger and death).
Baby birds nesting high in a cliff face will survive to fly through the world.
Moral: Babies that are not cared for properly are unfortunate (subject to illness and death).
Babies that are loved and cared for properly have a better chance of survival and success.
(Na Dr Hiko Te Rangi Hohepa (1993) in Pakai, 2004)

Consider part of the following philosophy as presented by Pakai (2004):

Early Childhood Care and Education is the basis of education for life. Children are our future,
therefore we are committed to support, value and nurture their growth and development, while
respecting their uniqueness, dignity, beliefs, ethnicity, culture, gender and ability.
http://reach.uvic.ca/PPT/Pakai_paper.pdf (accessed 9 February 2010)

All of the above provide further food for thought about the approaches to Early Years that we have in the UK, with subjects and philosophies to debate.

UK: EYFS Framework

Can the anxieties and reservations experienced in New Zealand be read as similar to the anxieties experienced by most of the Early Years workforce in the UK prior to the introduction of the EYFS Framework? Or was this anxiety linked more closely to the fact that there had been so many recent changes related to Early Years in the UK? The changes that the Early Years workforce has had to address have been the introduction of the following.

- Desirable Outcomes for Children's Learning on Entering Compulsory Education in 1996;
- Foundation Stage, with Desirable Learning Outcomes in 2000;
- The Desirable Learning Outcomes were then replaced by Early Learning Goals;
- Birth to Three Matters was introduced in November 2002;
- The Early Years Foundation Stage Framework, combining Birth to Three Matters and the Foundation Stage, became mandatory for Ofsted registered settings in September 2008.

Principles of the EYFS Framework

- **A Unique Child** – recognises that every child is a competent learner from birth who can be resilient, capable, confident and self- assured. The commitments are focused around development, inclusion, safety, and health and well-being.
- **Positive Relationships** – describes how children learn to be strong and independent from a base of loving and secure relationships with parents and/or a key person. The commitments are focused around respect; partnership with parents; supporting learning; and the role of the key person.
- **Enabling Environments** – explains that the environment plays a key role in supporting and extending children's development and learning. The commitments are focused around observation, assessment and planning; support for every child; the learning environment; and the wider context – transitions, continuity, and multi-agency working.
- **Learning and Development** – recognises that children develop and learn in different ways and at different rates, and that all areas of learning and development are equally important and inter-connected.

(EYFS Statutory Framework, 2008, p9)

ACTIVITY

Consider the four principles of the EYFS Framework and compare them with the principles of the Reggio Emilia approach and that of Te Whariki. Discuss the principles in detail. Are there strong similarities?

Now consider the experiences of Early Years children living in Eastern Europe that can be included within debates perhaps to strengthen the point that is being made about reading and writing and the commencement of compulsory schooling.

Eastern Europe

According to Horvath (2010), most children in Hungary start school at the age of seven, so most nursery Early Years provision is provided for children from the age of two to seven years. This is similar in Romania, Croatia, Slovakia, Bulgaria, the Czech Republic, Macedonia and Serbia, and while not researching communication, language and literacy specifically, Horvath (2010) does mention that the majority of children in Hungary who start school in September, aged seven, are able to read and write by December in the same year, again supporting the findings of Suggart (2009) that teaching children to read from the age of five does not appear to be of benefit. It is also very striking to note that in the above Eastern European countries the children start school at the earliest when they are six. In the majority of these countries the children learn through free play and only in Romania does it appear that children are taught formal writing, reading and maths.

School readiness

It is the practice in some countries to assess a child in order to decide whether they are ready to move from preschool to statutory school. Should a child demonstrate that they are not ready to move on to school the child, in consultation with the parents, will remain in preschool for an extra year. This is not seen as failure; it is viewed positively as a response to individual learning and developmental needs at that given time. The term 'school readiness' has been used in some instances (Al-Hassan and Lansford, 2009); this has not just been linked to the move to statutory schooling but also longer-term achievement. Al-Hassan and Lansford (2009) researched school readiness in Jordan and compared their findings with comparative research completed in North America and Europe. In all cases it was found that 'school readiness' was linked to the socio-economic status of the family and those from the families with lower incomes were less ready for school. Interestingly, though, and not related to economic status, the research in Jordan found that girls were less ready for school than boys. It was thought that this was linked to the culture in Jordan, where

> *Historically, boys in Jordan have been provided with more experiences that could enhance school readiness than have girls. For example, in Jordan girls are more often kept at home with their mothers, whereas boys are more often given the opportunity to explore their environments outside the home.*
>
> (Al-Hassan and Lansford, 2009)

Approaches to Early Years and primary curriculum

If we now return to consider the approach of the New Zealand government, to build upon the Early Childhood curriculum and the learning experiences that each child has already experienced it promotes discussion with regard to two recent reports written for the British Government.

- The Rose Report (2009).
- The Cambridge Primary Review (2009).

The reports both focus on the primary curriculum but also relate their findings to the EYFS Framework. In this chapter the links will be restricted to the impact of the EYFS Framework, the age to commence formal teaching of reading and writing, and the statutory school age.

The Rose Report

This report highlighted the need to broaden the primary curriculum and identified six areas of learning that 'dovetail' with the six areas of learning within the EYFS Framework, similar to the Te Whariki fitting with the primary curriculum and vice versa, in New Zealand. However, while providing material to debate, the Rose Report has not been taken forward by the current coalition government, which came into power after the general election in May 2010.

The six areas of learning recommended for the primary curriculum were:

- understanding English, communication and languages;
- mathematical understanding;
- scientific and technological understanding;
- historical, geographical and social understanding;
- understanding physical development, health and well-being;
- understanding the arts.

To refresh our memories and enable comparisons to be made, the six areas of learning for the EYFS Framework are:

- Personal, Social and Emotional Development;
- Communication, Language and Literacy;
- Problem Solving, Reasoning and Numeracy;
- Knowledge and Understanding of the World;
- Physical Development;
- Creative Development.

The following selection of recommendations from the Rose Report (2009) have been chosen for you to consider and to debate still further because they are directly linked to the EYFS Framework and also because they promote debate surrounding the age to teach reading and writing, and the age to enter compulsory schooling that we have been discussing in this chapter.

Recommendation 2

Consideration should be given to making the historically reactive response to curriculum review a proactive strategy whereby the EYFS and the statutory curriculum for primary and secondary schools are reviewed at agreed intervals as a whole, rather than as separate phases reviewed out of sequence. This would impose a discipline on the process of review such that schools could be assured of a period of stability in which to achieve agreed curricular goals.

(Rose, DSCF, 2009, p19)

Recommendation 10

(i) Primary schools should continue to build on the commendable progress many have made in teaching decoding and encoding skills for reading and spelling through high quality, systematic phonic work as advocated by the 2006 reading review 4 as the prime approach for teaching beginner readers.

(ii) Similar priorities and principles should apply to numeracy in keeping with the recommendations of the Williams Review.

(ibid., p22)

Recommendation 11

(i) The two early learning goals for writing should be retained as valid, aspirational goals for the end of the EYFS.

(ii) The DCSF should consider producing additional guidance for practitioners on supporting children's early writing and should offer practical examples of how this can work.

(ibid., p22)

Recommendation 14

(i) The preferred pattern of entry to reception classes should be the September immediately following a child's fourth birthday. However, this should be subject to well informed discussion with parents, taking into account their views of a child's maturity and readiness to enter reception class. Arrangements should be such as to make entry to reception class an exciting and enjoyable experience for all children, with opportunities for flexible arrangements such as a period of part-time attendance if judged appropriate.

(ii) The DCSF should provide information to parents and local authorities about the optimum conditions, flexibilities and benefits to children of entering reception class in the September immediately after their fourth birthday.

(ibid., p23)

Recommendation 17

Key Stage 1 teachers should be involved in the moderation of Early Years Foundation Stage Profile (EYFSP) assessments within schools, to increase their understanding of the EYFSP and their confidence in the judgements of reception class teachers.

(ibid., p24)

These recommendations support a child entering the Reception class within Primary schools at the age of four years.

The Cambridge Primary Review

In contrast to the Rose Report, the Cambridge Primary Review recommends extending the foundation stage to age six to build children's skills and confidence, and suggests that five is far too early for compulsory attendance as stated by an MP in 1870.

One has to ask the question, 'Why are we still having this debate given the findings of research and the European approach?'

ACTIVITY

Discuss these points in your groups. What is the majority consensus of opinion?

The key points taken from the Cambridge Primary Review that provide continuity of debate related to statutory school age and reading and writing are as follows:

- *Strengthen and extend early learning provision.*
- *Extend the foundation stage to age six.*
- *Replace KS1/2 with single primary phase from six to 11.*
- *Examine feasibility of raising school starting age to six.*
- *Have unified Early Years workforce strategy to raise quality of provision.*

(CPR booklet, 2009, p16)

The report speaks about protecting 'the distinctive nature of childhood' and the fact that, as learned from research, children need to flourish, to build social skills, language skills and confidence through the provision of structured play and opportunities for interaction with interested and stimulating adults.

The evidence is overwhelming that all children, but particularly those from disadvantaged homes, benefit from high-quality pre-school experiences.

(CPR booklet, 2009, p16)

Concerns are again raised about children entering school at the age of four who do not experience the areas of learning within the EYFS Framework through play and a well-provisioned learning environment.

ACTIVITY

Consider the above concern with your group. Does this reflect the practice in any of your settings? Is there any way that you can influence practice to ensure the EYFS Framework is delivered through rich play experiences?

To conclude this section of the chapter, the debate about the learning goals and assessment scales for communication, language and literacy and statutory school age is still on-going in the 'Open EYE' campaign.

ACTIVITY

Consider the following points within the assessment scale:
Linking Sounds and Letters:
  7. Uses phonic knowledge to read simple regular words.
  8. Attempts to read more complex words, using phonic knowledge.
  9. Uses knowledge of letters, sounds and words when reading and writing independently.

(EYFS Statutory Framework, 2008, p45)

Reading:
  6. Reads a range of familiar and common words and simple sentences independently.
  7. Retells narratives in the correct sequence, drawing on language patterns of stories.
  8. Shows an understanding of how information can be found in non-fiction texts to answer questions about where, who, why and how.
  9. Reads books of own choice with some fluency and accuracy.

Writing:
  7. Uses phonic knowledge to write simple regular words and make phonetically plausible attempts at more complex words.
  8. Begins to form captions and simple sentences, sometimes using punctuation.
  9. Communicates meaning through phrases and simple sentences with some consistency in punctuating sentences.

(EYFS Statutory Framework, 2008, p46)

In your experience, do many children reach these goals before moving to KS1? Find evidence to support your answers.

What are your views about these points of the assessment scale?

Inclusive Early Years provision

The EYFS also requires all settings to include children with special educational needs (SEN). However, inclusion in the broadest sense means inclusion for all, as explained in the quote from the EYFS Framework (see below). Inclusion when related to SEN alone raises many issues for some settings such as the physical environment, resources, how will the complex needs of the child be managed and is this setting the one that can provide for the best interests of the child? When Early Years Professionals feel challenged by the thought of inclusion, especially inclusion of children with complex needs, this is usually because they have, perhaps, fears that they will not be able to provide for these needs.

> • *Providing for equality of opportunity and anti-discriminatory practice and ensuring that every child is included and not disadvantaged because of ethnicity, culture or religion, home language, family background, learning difficulties of disabilities, gender or ability.*
>
> (EYFS Statutory Framework, 2008, p7)

This is expanded upon under the heading, 'Providing for equality of opportunity':

> *1.14 Providers have a responsibility to ensure positive attitudes to diversity and difference – not only that every child is included and not disadvantaged, but also so that they learn from the earliest age to value diversity in others and grow up making a positive contribution to society. Practitioners should focus on each child's individual learning, development and care needs by:*
>
> • *removing or helping to overcome barriers for children where these already exist;*
> • *being alert to the early signs of needs that could lead to later difficulties and responding quickly and appropriately, involving other agencies as necessary;*
> • *stretching and challenging all children.*
>
> (EYFS Statutory Framework, 2008, p9)

ACTIVITY

Having read the requirements of the EYFS Framework, consider what inclusion means to you. Have you ever felt excluded? How did you feel?

Discuss the above and write down your feelings. Then write your own definition of inclusion.

Here is a definition of inclusion in three parts, developed by a group of students having completed the above activity:

• To be welcomed, valued and respected as an individual to any group or part of society.
• To be treated fairly and equitably.
• To be able to adapt to changing situations and include the needs of each individual irrespective of difference.

Inclusion must be approached in its broadest sense to include everyone and not to always assume that it refers to children with SEN. It has been said that everyone experiences times in their lives when they have special needs. We can relate this to periods of transition; life events such as moving or immigrating; health – acute and chronic physical and mental illnesses. However, a learning disability is classified as one that is lifelong. In order to respond to individual needs to ensure inclusion, the EYP will ensure that regular observations are completed, meetings with parents are arranged to develop current learning and care plans, and to discuss the progression of the child to inform planning for future provision. Robinson (2010) cites Abbott and Langston (2005) regarding the responsibility of society to offer children with special needs and their families with maximum support and resources to manage the challenges involved.

The main initiatives and legislation, supporting and raising the profile of Early Years children with special needs, to develop the ethos of inclusion and the growth of integrated practice (Robinson, 2010) are:

- 1993 Education Act that includes the 1981 Education Act;
- 1994 SEN Code of Practice replaced by the 2001 SEN Code of Practice;
- Early Years Development and Childcare Plans/Partnerships;
- *Every Child Matters* (2003);
- *Removing Barriers to Achievement* (2004);
- *A Ten Year Strategy for Childcare* (2004);
- The Childcare Act (2006);
- Creation of Sure Start, now locally funded Children's Centres;
- Early Years Foundation Stage Framework (2008).

In contrast to the broad approach to inclusion in the UK, Italian nurseries (Reggio Emilia) and most other European countries, according to Phillips (2001), cited in Abbott and Nutbrown (2001), focus on severe and complex physical and learning difficulties. In Reggio Emilia (Phillips, 2001), this means children with an IQ of less than 65; those with severe physical disability, sensory impairment or emotional disturbance are included in their definition. In Italy, if a child with a severe disability attends a class, the number in the class is no more than 20 and there is specialist support. Phillips (2001) goes on to discuss early specialist intervention in the UK and the fact that it could result in the identification of a difference from other children. However, it could be argued that if all individual needs are responded to sensitively and every child is included and provided with an equal chance to succeed, the fact there are differences should be minimised. One could reflect here about the response of some adults to people with special needs; the response is sometimes inappropriate, whereas most young children embrace one another and do not notice differences. If they do, they will ask a question, hopefully receive an adequate explanation, and accept the child or adult and include them in the group.

The following overview of the *Index for Inclusion* (Booth et al., 2000, in Nutbrown, 2006) that has been specifically adapted for use Early Years Settings to enable settings to increase participation of all children in learning and play (www.csie.org.uk) may be helpful to explore in more detail. It illustrates the definition of inclusion in its broadest sense and supports the requirement for inclusive practice in the EYFS Framework.

The Index is aimed at all practitioners in these settings and builds on the widespread success in the UK and overseas of the 2004 edition.

- *The Index involves a self-review of all aspects of a setting, drawing on additional help as needed. It encourages the involvement in inclusive development of all practitioners, volunteers, management committee/governors, children, young people and their parents/carers.*
- *Resources for, and barriers to, play, learning and participation are identified during the Index process. Actions to assist inclusion are prioritised, and a development plan is drawn up, implemented and reviewed. These changes are sustained in the setting as the process is repeated.*
- *Within the Index process, practitioners are helped by 46 indicators of inclusion to investigate their culture, policy and practice and to combat all forms of discrimination. These are linked to over 600 questions which allow the setting to be reviewed in detail.*

(www.csie.org.uk)

Reading these through, for those who have not used the Index or any other form of quality tool, the process may appear very daunting. However, within the website (www.csie.org.uk) are comments that support the effectiveness of the process, for example, the children feel valued, everyone has been involved, the staff understand the needs of the parents and children, two-way communication has improved, management wish to develop the Index still further. So often when confronted with change that involves the introduction of new policies and practices the task appears enormous. However, once implemented, the changes enhance practice and experiences for all involved. Most importantly, all of the children will, for example, be able to participate in, learn from and enjoy the play experiences provided.

ACTIVITY

Discuss the outline of the *Inclusive Index* with your group. Consider the following:

- Have you implemented any parts of the Index?
- Would you be able to suggest implementing the Index to your management team?

The area of inclusion within Early Years settings, as with all aspects of childcare and education in the EYFS Framework, addresses many of the articles within the United Nations Convention on the Rights of the Child. This will now be visited, in brief, in the following paragraphs.

The United Nations Convention on the Rights of the Child

The United Nations Convention on the Rights of the Child was first adopted in 1989 by the United Nations General Assembly and was ratified by the UK in 1991. Each country has to develop policies relating to the 54 articles within the Convention. Compliance is monitored by a Committee for the Rights of the Child in Geneva. The rights of each child include:

- *the right to life, survival and development;*
- *the right to have their views respected, and to have their best interests considered at all times;*
- *the right to a name and nationality, freedom of expression, and access to information concerning them;*

- *the right to live in a family environment or alternative care, and to have contact with both parents wherever possible;*
- *health and welfare rights, including rights for disabled children, the right to health and health care, and social security;*
- *the right to education, leisure, culture and the arts;*
- *special protection for refugee children, children in the juvenile justice system, children deprived of their liberty and children suffering economic, sexual or other forms of exploitation.*

The rights included in the convention apply to all children and young people, with no exceptions.

www.direct.gov.uk/en/Parents/ParentsRights/DG_4003313

(accessed 9 February 2010)

As stated, there are 54 articles, which include those listed above; they are divided into categories under four main headings (Nutbrown, 2006): namely, prevention, provision, protection and participation.

The EYFS Framework states:

You must plan for each child's individual care and learning requirements. The focus should be on removing or helping to counter underachievement and overcoming barriers for children where these already exist. You should also identify and respond early to needs which could lead to the development of learning difficulties. There must be appropriate challenges for gifted and talented children.

(EYFS Practice Guidance 1 October, 2008, p6)

Within this section on meeting the diverse needs of children, the framework also includes promoting positive attitudes and understanding of diversity and difference to ensure that all feel valued and included, safe and secure. Thorough planning will ensure that due consideration is given to the promotion of positive attitudes and acknowledging the different first languages that may be spoken by some of the children and the different cultures they experience at home.

ACTIVITY

Consider the Rights of the Child above, read the full section in the EYFS Practice Guidance on meeting the diverse needs of children. Discuss the approach used in your setting. Write down areas of good practice and areas where practice could be improved. Which other theories could be used to support your work?

Inclusion continues to promote debate, although it would appear that the benefits of inclusion are positive for all the children, parents and staff involved in Early Years settings. This leads into the last section of this chapter with a short investigation of gender issues when employing staff because inclusion/equality of opportunity relates to staff as well as children and parents.

Staff gender issues in Early Years

It is a well-known and reported fact that the workforce in Early Years is female dominated. This is across the board of maintained, private and voluntary Early Years settings and primary schools in the UK. Why is this? Is it because of poor pay? Is it because of poor working conditions? Is it because of a lack of career progression? Is it historic? Is it cultural and because women had, until recently, been seen as the carer in the family context with the man being the 'hunter gatherer' and hence the parent who went out of the home to provide for the family? This characteristic of families has prevailed throughout time in the UK, except when there has been the need for women to work. This is supported by information in Chapter 2 on the history of the Early Years where it can be seen that the development of the provision of childcare corresponded to, for example, each of the world wars when women were required to work to replace many of the men who had gone to fight in the wars, in order to keep the economy moving forward and ensure supplies of vital commodities. In more recent times it has, as we know, corresponded to the demographic change in the UK for women to return to work following the birth of their child/children rather than to stay at home and care for their children until they are of school age. Some children would attend a nursery school or preschool from three to five years of age in the mornings and if a mother had to work, for financial reasons, there were a few day-care settings available. The requirement for women to return to work more recently has not only been linked to financial necessity but also to support industry and fill job vacancies. There are many more opportunities for women to study, qualify, develop and continue their careers that had not been available in the past.

Addressing equality of opportunity has resulted in opportunities to access and continue in further and higher education for all. There are opportunities in every career for all, whether male or female. However, we still need to explore employment statistics to assess the impact on access to gender-dominated professions. Women are employed, for example, in engineering, building and medicine, whereas these areas were always male dominated. It could be argued that they still are, as Henty (2009) quoted from an article in the *Education Guardian* that women have to be brave to enter a building site. This example could also be related to physical ability – men are generally physically stronger than women. However, we can relate having to feel brave to enter a male-dominated domain to that of men having to feel brave to enter the female-dominated domain of Early Years. Medicine and nursing have been, respectively, male and female dominated in the past. The situation is changing, as can be seen in the information below for medicine, which shows that women now account for 40 per cent of the workforce. Whereas the change in nursing is less dramatic, the number of men in the workforce is between 10 and 11 per cent. Again, is this because nursing is a caring profession and not seen as a male domain?

ACTIVITY

Consider the number of men who were on your level 3 courses, the number who are on your Foundation Degree and the number employed in your setting. Discuss this in your groups. Add the number of men and women employed across the settings in your group and then work out the percentage of men employed.

Table 6.2: Employment in the UK (April–June 2008) by status, occupation and sex

ALL IN EMPLOYMENT BY STATUS, OCCUPATION AND SEX, Quarter 2 (April – June) 2008	Total in employment, UK, not seasonally adjusted	Men in employment	Women in employment	Total employees, full-time	Total employees, part-time
Medical practitioners	214,122	115,245	98,877	143,412	23,112
Nurses	527,992	56,718	471,274	336,486	188,841
Prim and nurs education teaching profs	392,454	54,658	337,796	289,456	99,128
Nursery nurses	155,167	*	153,393	87,946	61,788
Childminders and rel occupations	130,357	*	125,934	20,420	28,973
Playgroup leaders and assistants	50,206	*	46,234	14,182	34,912

Adapted from spreadsheets on www.google.com – accessed 14 February 2010.

Here is adapted data from other countries in Europe, in comparison with England and Scotland, accessed on the website www.ltscotland.org.uk/earlyyears.

- England has set targets of 6 per cent men in employment by 2004; Owen (2003) shows that men still only make up 1per cent of the childcare workforce.
- Scotland statistics show that men only make up 2 per cent of the childcare workforce.

While

- in Denmark, men make up 3 per cent of the pedagogical workforce;
- Norway has achieved almost 10 per cent men in the workforce;
- in Belgium, male trainees increased from 6.5 per cent to 20 per cent following a recruitment campaign;
- Poland has almost no male workers.

It would appear that campaigns to recruit men into training and the workforce do help to raise the number of men choosing childcare as a career. However, Denmark, Norway, Sweden and Belgium identify the fact that campaigning needs to be continuous; if not, the number of men entering the profession drops and in some cases decreases right back to original numbers, as was found in Belgium.

Andrews and Bayliss (2009) identified the lack of research into reasons why men do not choose to go into childcare. Is it because, as spoken about earlier, they have to be brave? Is it linked to cultural perceptions that child-caring is not for men, even when fathers are more involved in the day-to-day care and education of their children? Is it, again suggested by Andrews and Bayliss (2009), linked to the safeguarding agenda? The safeguarding agenda promotes many emotions, particularly when providing personal care for very young children, such as nappy changing. However, it must be remembered that it is not just men who abuse children, women do too. This fact was only too apparent when a woman was jailed for having abused and taken pornographic pictures of children in the nursery where she was employed in 2009. In practice, it is important to safeguard children, to be aware of our roles within childcare and education, to ensure all staff members are employed using the 'safer recruitment' process and to ensure that everyone employed in the setting has an enhanced CRB check.

Is it beneficial to the children to employ men in Early Years and if so, why and how? Many would answer that they provide a role model for the children, particularly boys. Nilsen and Manum (1998) cited in Cameron et al. (1999) see men opening up opportunities for exploration and outdoor play which they value more than women – a good link to the EYFS and outdoor play. They also thought that men caring for children could impact on fathers, helping the next generation of fathers to be more caring. Jensen (1996) concludes that:

Getting men into childcare is a long process that will not happen overnight . . .

The main reason to get more men into childcare services is that it will improve the quality of the childcare services and play a part in supporting equal opportunities for girls and boys in these services.

(Jensen, 1996, p53)

Jensen (1996) also speaks about the provision of quality childcare and education that fully responds to individual needs of both boys and girls, and that this can best be delivered by a well-qualified staff team that includes both men and women. This is considering provision holistically, not just the day-to-day activities but the whole environment with its resources, human and physical (both indoors and outdoors), where everyone is respected and valued.

In this brief exploration of staff gender issues in Early Years it would appear that the issues are complex. However, a recruitment campaign or setting up an organisation such as that in Edinburgh called 'Men in Childcare' might begin to alter the male/female imbalance that exists in the childcare and education workforce.

ACTIVITY
Discuss ways of drawing men into childcare and education.

In conclusion, this chapter has been written to introduce and explore some of the different debates that are on-going within the childcare and education sector. Our society continues to change at an enormous pace, prompting further debates on the effect that aspects of this may have on children. For example, should the subject of ICT, which changes very quickly with faster and faster access to websites through advances in technology, be available in nurseries? Should children in day-care settings be allowed to watch television? The list is exhaustive.

The expectations of Early Years workers can seem overwhelming at times – being expected to respond to constant change and to remain positive is one of the major challenges. Early Years workers also have to respond continuously to the changing needs of the children, the changing wishes of parents, the changes in legislation and the demands of increased bureaucracy.

However, whatever the debate, we must always remember each individual child. The child must remain at the centre of all we do. Learn, observe, reflect, discuss, plan, work with other professionals, work with parents, work with your immediate team, implement *Always keeping the child at the centre*.

CHAPTER SUMMARY

- This chapter has asked you to participate in some of the current debates around Early Years practice.
- It has looked at the EYFS in comparison with some international perspectives on education and specifically on the ages at which children are expected to start their formal education.
- The chapter then explored the concept of inclusion and what it means for education before finally exploring the dearth of males in the childcare sector.

Chapter 7 offers a conclusion to the book by debating where you go once you have completed your FD, ways in which you can achieve EYPS and what this actually means in terms of the skills you will need to acquire. It looks at the importance of being a creative practitioner and of you devoting yourself to your own CPD in order to become an effective leader.

REFERENCES
Abbott, L and Nutbrown, C (Editors) (2001) *Experiencing Reggio Emilia*. Buckingham: Open University Press.

Al-Hassan, SM and Lansford, JE (2009) Child Family and Community Characteristics Associated with School Readiness in Jordan, in TACTYC, *Early Years, an International Journal of Research and Development*, Vol. 29, No. 3, Oct 2009, Abingdon: Routledge.

Andrews, M and Bayliss, S (2009) Male Status Symbols, in *Early Years Educator*, Vol. 11, No. 3, July 2009. London: MA Education.

Cameron, C, Moss, P and Owen, C (1999) *Men in the Nursery.* London: Paul Chapman Publishing.

DCSF (2008) *Statutory Framework for the Early Years Foundation Stage*. Nottingham: DCSF Publications.

DCSF (2008) *Practice Guidance for the Early Years Foundation Stage*. Nottingham: DCSF Publications.

Gandini, L and Pope Edwards, C (Editors) (2001) *Bambini: The Italian Approach to Infant/Toddler Care*. London: Teachers College Press.

Hawkins, D (1998) Remarks: Malaguzzi's Story, Other Stories, in Edwards, C, Gandini, L and Forman, G *The Hundred Languages of Children: The Reggio Emilia Approach – Advance Reflections*. 2nd edition. London: Ablex Publishing.

Henty, N (2009) Paths to the Future, in *Early Years Educator*, Vol. 11, No. 5, Sept. 2009. London: MA Education.

Horvath, J (2010) Through Another's Eyes, in *Early Years Educator*, Vol. 11, No. 11, March 2010. London: MA Education.

Jensen, J (1996) *Men as Workers in Childcare Services – A Discussion* London, ECNC, Thomas Coram Research Unit.

Moss, P, Petrie, P (2002) *From Children's Services to Children's Spaces*. London: Routledge.

Nutbrown, C (2006) *Key Concepts in Early Childhood Education and Care*. London: Sage.

Nuttal, J (2003) *Weaving Te Whariki*. New Zealand: New Zealand Council for Educational Research.

Pugh, G and Duffy, B (2010) (Editors) *Contemporary Issues in the Early Years* (5th edition). London: Sage.

Rose, J (2009) *Independent Review of the Primary Curriculum: Final Report*. Nottingham: DCSF Publications.

FURTHER READING

Blandford, S and Knowles, C (2009) *Developing Professional Practice 0–7*. Harlow: Pearson Education.

Edwards, C, Gandini, L Forman, G (1998) *The Hundred Languages of Children*. 2nd edition. New Jersey: Ablex Publishing.

Yelland, N (1998) *Gender Issues in Early Childhood*. London: Routledge.

WEBSITES

www.csie.org.uk/publications/index-early-summary.shtml (accessed 10 February 2010).

www.direct.gov.uk/en/Parents/ParentsRights/DG_4003313 (accessed 10 February 2010).

http://ecrp.uiuc.edu/v10n2/gilbert.html (accessed 10 February 2010).

http://www.eric.ed.gov/ERICDocs/data/ericdocs2sql/content_storage_01/0000019b/80/14/da/71.pdf

http://www.ltscotland.org.uk/earlyyears/about/currentissues/maleworkers/aboutmaleworkers.asp (accessed 14 February 2010).

http://madrid.angloinfo.com/countries/spain/toddlers.asp (accessed 8 February 2010).

http://www.meninchildcare.co.uk/Mens%20Work.pdf (accessed 8 February 2010).

http://openeyecampaign.wordpress.com/2009/09/02/the-early-years-foundation-stage-%E2%80%93-one-year-on (accessed 8 February 2010).

http://spreadsheets.google.com/pub?key=r3na8bY1NAbSbXNYtPmwVuw&output=html (accessed 14 February 2010).

7 THE FUTURE: EARLY YEARS PROFESSIONAL STATUS

CHAPTER OBJECTIVES

By the end of this chapter you will:

- have considered what's next now you've completed your Foundation Degree;
- appreciate the importance of Continuing Professional Development (CPD);
- have a wonderful knowledge of the EYP standards;
- have reflected on what the future holds for the Early Years sector.

Introduction

This chapter looks forward to the role of the EYP in the future, imagining a sector where professionals work in partnership with others, often in centres where children and family services are brought together on one site, led by staff who have completed their degrees and have continued their professional development, thus allowing them to take a leadership role of multi-professional teams. This chapter has clear links to Chapter 4 'Becoming an Early Years Professional'.

What's next now you've finished your Foundation Degree?

Having spent two years and made lots of sacrifices to successfully achieve your FD, you will feel 'the world is your oyster', but what can you actually do with it? Everyone told you that having a degree was one of the best things you could do as it would make you more 'employable'.

People who have degrees are generally viewed by employers as having good motivation, staying power, problem-solving skills; the ability to write well, and so on.

Here is what Jane, a recent FD student, has to say:

> *The Foundation Degree has affected my life in a number of ways. I am in absolutely no doubt whatsoever that the knowledge and skills that the Foundation Degree brings have afforded me the rite of passage to a senior role within the company. In doing the Foundation Degree, I've acquired some fantastic skills and knowledge that will take me forward in my current role and my future career.*

Further benefits are that this student now believes in herself, the FD has given her confidence and she believes that her opinions are now valued and worth listening to. As her lecturer I know that when she started the course she often felt intimidated by other professionals and thought she had less worth than them. Clearly, this has all changed and she is able to act as an advocate for children in her care when representing their interests at multi-agency meetings.

Once Jane had completed her FD, she decided to continue to study and went on to complete a BA Honours degree graduating with a First in July 2009. Jane sums up by saying:

> *The 'foundation' in Foundation Degree means exactly what it says – it gave me an excellent foundation to go on to further study.*

She believes the quality of the education received on the course went a long way to helping her achieve a First. Since qualifying, Jane has been promoted to a managerial position at her nursery with operational responsibility for the day-to-day running of the centre.

Early Years Professional Status (EYPS)

It is generally agreed that Early Years services are better when they are led by graduate practitioners, EYPs, who reflect on their practice to improve what they do, and who guide and support others to be the best they can be. The CWDC developed, in collaboration with many Early Years practitioners, an extensive list of standards for EYPs to achieve to ensure they are providing the best quality care for children that they can.

If you are working in an Early Years setting and see this as your future, you may want to consider gaining the above status. There are four pathways to achieving this.

Depending on your previous experience, you will be eligible for either:

- the four-month part-time validation programme;
- the six-month part-time short extended professional development (EPD) pathway;
- the twelve-month full-time training pathway.

If you have an Early Years Foundation Degree (Level 5) or an equivalent qualification, you will be eligible for the long EPD pathway, which lasts 15 months, and be able to top up to a full degree during the programme (CWDC, 2010).

To gain EYPS you must be a graduate who can demonstrate that you meet a set of national, professional Standards when working with children from birth to five. The Standards set out the knowledge, understanding, skills and other professional attributes that an EYP will need. It is the government's aim to have EYPs in all Children's Centres offering Early Years provision by 2010 and in every full day-care setting by 2015.

The EYP Standards

The Standards are organised under six related headings that describe the criteria for attaining EYPS:

- Knowledge and understanding.
- Effective practice.
- Relationships with children.
- Communicating and working in partnership with families and carers.
- Teamwork and collaboration.
- Professional development.

The Standards are accompanied by guidance which illustrates the type of activities and responsibilities undertaken by the EYP; sets out the scope of each Standard; provides examples of how each Standard can be demonstrated in different settings and with babies, toddlers and young children; and gives examples of the ways in which evidence can be used to support Standards that are closely linked. This helps:

- assessors to make consistent judgements against the Standards;
- trainers to develop programmes which enable candidates to meet the Standards;
- candidates to understand what is expected of them and how they might demonstrate that they meet the Standards;
- employers to know what they can expect of newly qualified EYPs and which of their existing staff might be encouraged to work towards gaining EYPS.

As the CWDC website tells us:

Early Years is a dynamic and vitally important sector which needs high quality staff at all levels. Those who work in it play a crucial role in shaping the lives of future generations. It is a career that you can rightly be very proud of.

EYPs will:

- work as part of the team of skilled and committed people working with children in Early Years settings or wider children's services;
- take responsibility for leading and managing play, care and learning;

- have a secure and up-to-date knowledge and understanding of Early Years practice with children from birth to five;
- be skilled and effective practitioners.

In addition to this, EYPs will have an important role in leading and supporting other staff by helping them to develop and improve their practice, establish and maintain positive relationships with children and communicate and work in partnership with families, carers and other professionals. Clearly, in order to achieve all this, EYP need to have certain personal qualities and one of the key abilities that will enable them to do this is that of creativity.

The creative practitioner

Each of us is made up of the sum of our lifelong experiences, but as the government says in *Children's Plan: Building Brighter Futures* (2007), what society needs is a workforce that can promote creativity and communication. If, as EYPs, we feel able to be creative ourselves, we will be able to promote it in our team; the setting will then feel able to encourage children to be creative.

This will have a 'knock-on' effect, not only improving children's ability to learn but also to rise to challenging and interesting situations therefore promoting the emotional resilience needed for the five key aims of ECM, to:

- be healthy;
- stay safe;
- enjoy and achieve;
- make a positive contribution;
- achieve economic well-being.

The qualities needed to be a creative practitioner able to encourage and promote creativity in those around them are many and include enthusiasm, a willingness and ability to 'think outside the box' and to be optimistic. This is only possible in an environment where there is a culture of learning, dialogue, reflection and communication. There also needs to be an acceptance that there will be some errors where there is risk taking. An open, supportive culture will value divergent thinking and creative responses, therefore reducing the stress around innovation and embracing change as part of its creative process.

One of the more important roles of the EYP is helping the setting to move on and make changes to daily routines that will positively affect the children in their care and encourage them to try imaginative solutions.

The strength of all Early Years settings lies in the creativity, expertise and experience of the practitioners who work there. Being a creative practitioner involves being enthusiastic, seeing the potential in interesting and unusual situations, and coping with uncertainty. Creative practitioners understand the importance of developing a physical and emotional environment where children feel confident to explore and investigate, finding things out for themselves.

Working creatively with young children is an exciting and challenging job, which requires particular personal and professional skills, taking on different roles depending on the age group of the children or the requirements of the parents, colleagues or professional partners you are interacting with. All these aspects require you to be able to respond to different situations by acting as a motivator, communicator, expert or organiser as the situation demands it.

> **ACTIVITY**
> To illustrate what these different roles might look like in practice, think about a situation you have encountered recently where you have attempted to help a parent find a solution to a child's problematic behaviour.

Thornton and Brunton (2009) pointed out the following.

In your role as a **motivator** you may well be involved in encouraging the parent to believe she is capable of resolving the behaviour issue. You will listen carefully to the ideas put forward by the parent and encourage them to think of sensible solutions.

As a **communicator**, you may be consulting with colleagues (with the parent consent) to ensure they are aware of the situation and what the family is attempting to achieve so that they can also support them. This involves listening to what everyone has to say, sharing ideas with all colleagues in the setting to keep them informed and involved.

As the **expert**, the knowledgeable adult, you will have ideas about the best way to achieve a positive change. You will use your knowledge of child development to help the parent select the best course of action.

Good organisation is the key to the success of any project. In your role as an **organiser** you will be making sure the appropriate information is available both for parents and for colleagues you are working with.

Continuing professional development and Early Years professionals

What are the benefits of CPD?

- CPD will have an impact on standards and motivation levels. You will feel a sense of achievement when you have acquired new skills and grow in confidence to take more responsibility.
- Training has many spin-offs and related advantages. With enhanced confidence and enthusiasm, you are more likely to be innovative and able to develop new ways of doing things. You are also more likely to 'see the bigger picture' and think strategically about the nursery, its services and development.
- Going on training courses will give you the opportunity to share experiences, thus gaining from others' ideas, and to maintain a support network of like-minded professionals working in similar settings.

- You also have the knowledge that you are doing your best to be open to new ideas and are staying up-to-date with current thinking in your field.

However, it may feel that achieving EYPS was the pinnacle of your aspirations. After all, you may already know that you want to carry on working in an Early Years setting and you have a degree, so why should you consider engaging in any more study?

Further study will help you in your daily work because:

- it will produce a more competent and capable workforce;
- by sharing your skills with others, you will free yourself to do other tasks;
- you will be able to share the workload and achieve more by involving other team member;
- team members will become more motivated and enthusiastic;
- individuals will appreciate the investment you are making and stay with you because they feel challenged.

We are now living in a culture of lifelong learning and constant change. It is not possible to sit back and to consider yourself fully qualified and in no more need of further knowledge. Another key point is that children learn from adults and they are more likely to engage in learning where there is a culture of enjoyment in learning being passed down from the adults caring for them.

The concept of lifelong learning needs to be an integral part of an organisation's activities and ethos. From the person at the top to the most part-time member of staff, CPD needs to be seen as an important and significant way to raise standards, keep staff and nurture potential.

You can sense a nursery's atmosphere, good or bad, when you walk in. An environment where staff are motivated, happy, lively, enthusiastic and keen, is almost always a sign that they feel cared for and respected. This will be a place where parents will feel happy to leave their children. Taking the time to keep your skills and knowledge updated and training your staff will also increase skills and levels of professionalism and this too will create a positive reputation for the nursery.

Key areas of CPD that are common to all Early Years workers

- **Action research.** Think of all those observations you do and what you learn from them. It only needs a short leap for you to go one step further and to think about how you could structure them into a research strategy designed to answer some burning question you have about child behaviour.
- **Reflection.** A key aspect of the EYP role, used as a way of informing practice and improving the quality of the care you are giving. This needs to be on-going throughout your career and the evidence stored in your professional portfolio, for you and colleagues to refer back to when you feel the need.
- **Leadership skills.** EYPs acting as leaders and change agents is a primary part of their role. Developing this fully and maintaining a sense of currency depends not only on developing the skills by gaining practical experience, but also having the opportunity to discuss and explore those experiences with others in similar situations (Pound, 2008).

- **Mentoring.** An important aspect of leadership is supporting and helping colleagues in their professional development and this is highlighted well as a leader takes on the role of mentoring other staff.

The future of Early Years

Salaries

Despite the government's £350m Graduate Leader Fund (GLF), which can help to cover additional costs for settings that want to employ an EYPS or train an existing member of staff, average salaries remain low in comparison to other graduate professions, and with no central pay structure for Early Years workers there can be a big disparity between salaries in different settings.

Day settings are among the hardest hit. While most are supportive of the changes, and keen to increase salaries for better qualified staff, increasing fees for parents is their one option and one most cannot afford to take.

The National Day Nurseries Association, which represents 3,000 organisations, says nurseries in the private and voluntary sectors are reporting that they cannot match the pay offered elsewhere. The CWDC admits there is no magic solution but says they are in discussions with the Department for Children, Schools and Families (DCSF) to develop CPD opportunities for EYPS, along similar lines to the teaching profession, where more specialised roles have been introduced allowing teachers to further develop their careers.

There is also evidence that graduates with EYPS are moving from the private and voluntary settings to Children's Centres and elsewhere, where salaries are higher; it is an issue that has been taken up by the CWDC, which is tracking the destinations of EYPS. In the next five years the number of graduates working in Early Years is set to rise to 20,000, so having made a lot of investment in Early Years to raise the level of qualifications, it has made none in improving pay levels and that needs to happen to encourage EYPS to stay in Early Years or the investment will be wasted.

Developing a code of conduct

One of the problems of having Early Years practitioners working in such a wide range of settings with different funding sources is that there has been no overall body co-ordinating pay and conditions as there is in nursing or teaching. This has meant that Early Years practitioners have developed their own codes of conduct for working with children and families in Early Years settings. Of course, many settings have their own philosophy of childcare prominently displayed and implicit in all their policies, but this ad hoc approach is not good enough for a developing profession and may be an area that the CWDC will focus on in the coming years.

Australia and New Zealand have both successfully developed robust codes designed to act as guidance to staff in Early Years settings and they generally adhere to the following principles:

Personal integrity
We act with care and diligence and make decisions that are honest, fair, impartial, and timely, and consider all relevant information.

Relationships with others

We treat people with respect, courtesy and sensitivity and recognise their interests, rights, safety and welfare.

Accountability

We use the resources of the state in a responsible and accountable manner that ensures the efficient, effective and appropriate use of human, natural, financial and physical resources, property and information.

Some key values that ought to be incorporated into a code of professional conduct are as follows:
- *Respect the dignity, worth, and uniqueness of each individual (child, family member, and colleague).*
- *Respect diversity in children, families, and colleagues.*
- *Recognise that children and adults achieve their full potential in the context of relationships that are based on trust and respect.*
- *Appreciate childhood as a unique and valuable stage of the human life cycle.*
- *Base our work on knowledge of how children develop and learn.*
- *Appreciate and support the bond between the child and family.*
- *Recognise that children are best understood and supported in the context of family, culture, community and society.*

(New Zealand early childhood curriculum, 1996)

The Australian code enshrines the following principle as the most important:

- *Above all, we shall not harm children. We shall not participate in practices that are disrespectful, degrading, dangerous, exploitative, intimidating, emotionally damaging or physically harmful to children.*

(www.earlychildhoodaustralia.org.au/, accessed 12 February 2010)

Until recently, in the UK we had the Children's Workforce Network, which was 'an alliance committed to creating and supporting a world-class children's workforce in England'. The organisation was a strategic body, bringing together the relevant Sector Skills Councils (including the CWDC) and other partners. It was, however, a voluntary grouping of independent partners, who recognised that collaboration would help them to achieve the more effective implementation of their individual and joint roles.

The Network's vision was a children's workforce that:

- supports integrated and coherent services for children, young people and families;
- remains stable and appropriately staffed, while exhibiting flexibility and responsiveness;
- is trusted and accountable, and thereby valued;
- demonstrates high skills, productivity and effectiveness;
- exhibits strong leadership, management and supervision.

Much of their work has been taken up by the Alliance of Sector Skills Councils and, of course, both the CWDC and DCSF will have a strong role to play in ensuring different sectors of childcare work together to develop common philosophies to guide their work with children.

ACTIVITY

What sorts of things would you want to see in a Code of Ethics for your profession?

Explore under these headings:

- In relation to children, I will:
- In relation to families, I will:
- In relation to colleagues, I will:
- In relation to communities, I will:
- In relation to students, I will:
- In relation to my employer, I will:
- In relation to myself as a professional, I will:
- In relation to the conduct of research, I will:

The development of Children's Centres

Social services, Children's Centres and extended schools in every local community must work together across professional boundaries to provide integrated childcare and Early Years education to ensure that all children get the services and support that are tailored to their needs. The government's focus on Early Years and education is driven by its concern to reduce child poverty and disadvantage. It believes that paid work (and therefore non-parent childcare) is the only route out of poverty.

In July 1998 a White Paper entitled *Modern Public Services for Britain* was published. It made a recommendation that new Children's Services should be introduced. It was hoped these services would be multifaceted in nature and improve the lives of children and parents from areas in need of these types of services.

This was followed up by a Green Paper, *Meeting the Childcare Challenge*, also in 1998, which set out the National Childcare Strategy, and subsequently the *Every Child Matters* Green Paper in 2003.

Originally, it was intended that there would be 250 Sure Start Local Programmes by March 2002. However, following early success, a ten-year strategy for childcare, published in December 2004, pledged that by March 2010 there would be a Children's Centre in every community.

A successful start

With the March 2010 deadline now past, Children's Centres are present in many communities and there is a drive to ensure that these centres are made as successful as possible. This includes launching initiatives to promote awareness of what they are doing, utilising the resources available at these centres and, at the same time, making sure the community is aware of what extensive help and support they have right on their doorstep.

Much of the evaluation into the success of the centres may only become possible once a generation has passed through their doors, but early research into their progress has produced some positive results. For instance, a 2008 report by Ofsted into the progress of Children's Centres showed that the services delivered to the community had a very positive effect on the lives of the children and parents, and many of the users felt the services on offer were very valuable.

Further, a more recent Ofsted report published in July 2009 showed that the successes were continuing, stating that *nearly all of the centres had established an effective balance between providing integrated services that are open to everyone and those that are targeted towards potentially vulnerable families.*

As the Every Child Matters website says:

> *Sure Start Children's Centres have been developed as hubs where children under five years old and their families can receive seamless integrated services and information. By 2010, every community will be served by a Sure Start Children's Centre, offering permanent universal provision across the country, ensuring that every child gets the best start in life.*
>
> *These services vary according to centre but may include:*

- *integrated early education and childcare – all centres offering Early Years provision have a minimum half-time qualified teacher (increasing to full-time within 18 months of the centre opening);*
- *support for parents – including advice on parenting, local childcare options and access to specialist services for families;*
- *child and family health services – ranging from health screening, health visitor services to breast-feeding support;*
- *helping parents into work – with links to the local Jobcentre Plus and training.*

(www.dcfs.gov.uk/everychildmatters/earlyyears/surestart)

A new government

In May 2010, a coalition government between the Conservatives and the Liberal Democrats was announced. It is difficult to foretell how this will affect the Early Years sector; however, we can see that there are some definite areas that the two parties agree on and some others that will cause a degree of compromise and, of course, all debates over children's and youth policy need to be considered against the deep shadow of public spending cuts.

Here are some of their areas of consensus and conflict, as identified by Chandiramani (2010).

Areas of consensus

Child poverty

All parties are committed in principle to eradicate child poverty by 2020. The education system provides one of the key mechanisms by which to achieve this for both Tories and Liberal Democrats. David Cameron has cited the 'pupil premium' as a key policy on which they could agree. This would act as an incentive by directing payments to state schools for each pupil from a disadvantaged background whom they admit. The scale of the commitment will be a matter for debate – the Liberal Democrats earmarked £2.5bn to fund the policy in their manifesto, £1.5bn of which would come from tax rises for the highest earners.

Families and parenting

The parties are united in their desire to extend shared parental leave when a child is born and therefore in their conviction that the love and care that children receive in their early life is of critical importance. They also both believe in extending the right to flexible working for all parents.

Child protection

Both the Conservatives and the Liberal Democrats want to publish in full the serious case reviews when a child dies as a result of abuse or neglect.

They both also want to scrap the ContactPoint information sharing database. While the Tories say they would replace it with a signposting system for 'genuinely vulnerable children', the Liberal Democrats say they would use the savings from its abolition to offer administrative and technical support to social workers.

Early Years and childcare

Both parties are sceptical about the EYFS curriculum for under-fives. The Conservatives have said that while retaining it, they want to cut the bureaucracy it involves, while the Liberal Democrats favour a slimmed-down curriculum.

AREAS OF CONFLICT

Joint working

Here, the Tories want some degree of retreat, while the Liberal Democrats want to go the other way and bring in plans to deepen integrated working.

The Conservatives regard Labour's *Every Child Matters* reforms as fine in principle, but they regard the joint working arrangements that it has brought about as overly bureaucratic in practice. So they want to repeal the obligations on local areas to have children's trusts in place and for local authorities to publish children and young people's plans.

The Liberal Democrats, by contrast, want to strengthen joint working arrangements so that housing authorities have a duty to co-operate in children's trusts, which would compel housing professionals and planners to consider the interests and welfare of children in their decision making. They also propose that practitioners have secondments in other areas of children's services, so that for example, a children's social worker gains experience of the challenges of being a youth worker and vice versa.

Families and parenting

The Conservatives' proposal to reward marriage in the tax system is likely to sit uneasily with a party that is meant to be inherently 'liberal' in its instinct and uncomfortable about an endorsement and incentive of one form of family life above another.

Schools

Aside from their shared support for the pupil premium, it is unclear how much the Liberal Democrats would be willing to support Michael Gove's radical proposals for state-funded schools to be allowed freedom from local authorities and for more academies to be established. Indeed, the Liberal Democrats want to replace academies with so-called 'sponsor-managed schools' that would still be accountable to local authorities.

Sure Start Children's Centres

The Conservatives want Sure Start to revert to its original purpose of targeting disadvantaged families. This prompted Labour before and during the election campaign to pronounce that there would be a drastic retreat in availability of Sure Start services under a Tory government.

However, while the Tories plan to redirect funds from Sure Start outreach workers to create an extra 4,200 health visitors, the Liberal Democrats favour focusing resources on improving outreach services. They do not appear to share the Tories' scepticism about the effectiveness of outreach workers, and they are clear that though they see the value of having more health visitors in place, they are working with limited resources and so this may have to be part of a longer-term plan.

Leading into the future

We must be the change we wish to see.

Mahatma Gandhi

How true this is! It is just what the government ordered when it developed the idea of the EYPS. You are engaging in the journey of a new profession with all the pitfalls and setbacks that you have observed in other professions. You are expected to be the leaders in this new profession and all of the issues and dilemmas of the future outlined above will be yours to solve.

One of the key challenges of the future will be endeavouring to work with the wide range of professionals that are involved in working with children in multi-agency teams. The Department of Health project *Creating an Interprofessional Workforce (CIPW)* developed 'effective leadership' grids that identified four key elements of an interprofessional workforce.

- Leaders are fully aware of the big picture.
- Leaders have a vision for change.
- Leaders have the ability to build a shared vision while fostering creativity and innovation.
- Leaders work with partners to develop strategies for collaborative working.

It is important that you pay attention to the big picture so that you are well equipped to lead your setting into the future, knowing that you have planned for every eventuality and that your staff and the children and families in your care will not suffer because you had not foreseen events that may have an impact on them. One issue that springs to mind here is the redirection of resources that may occur with the previously outlined change of government, Early Years care and education is not a key emphasis for all the political parties and the Early Years sector may find itself suffering a shortage of funds if those resources take a change of direction.

Seeing the bigger picture does not just mean seeing the threats to ways of working but also seeing these as a challenge to change – after all, it is change that makes us creative in our work.

Selling a vision to our staff can sometimes be daunting, but each setting needs to work as a cohesive team with a shared vision if it is to survive. If a team is not creative about finding solutions, it will quickly become stale and lack motivation for the day-to-day work.

Working with partners means finding out about their concerns, motivations and roles, and sharing ideas with them for the benefit of clients. Each partner brings its own language, philosophies and priorities, which will build on those sets of skills and knowledge already present to form a new and better whole.

The government is putting an increased emphasis on inter-agency working. Early Years practitioners, particularly those with a leadership role, will be instrumental in developing and putting policy into practice as it evolves. Building and developing an effective integrated team will mean developing traditional roles for the new challenges of integrated working, breaking down cultural barriers and managing change. The leader, be it of a Children's Centre or a nursery setting, will have a key role to play in shaping and structuring these individuals from diverse backgrounds into a team.

The role of the EYP is to be a *catalyst for change and innovation* (CWDC, 2008, p5). However, though practitioners may be committed to the idea of a cohesive service for families, the reality of working in this way will demand huge changes professionally and psychologically. It takes a great deal of sensitivity, creativity, enthusiasm and patience to encourage teams to move on and accept the changes, especially as colleagues try to cling to old ways of doing things, not seeing that there has been a cultural change that necessitates doing things differently (McKimm et al., 2009).

Creating new leaders

One final demand of EYPs is that they work with their colleagues to support them in engaging in more study; mentoring is one such strategy that may be used to develop more leaders.

Mentoring is a relationship between two people with the goal of professional and personal development. The 'mentor' is usually an experienced individual who shares knowledge, experience and advice with a less experienced person, or 'mentee'. A mentor affects the professional life of a protégé by fostering insight, identifying needed knowledge and expanding growth opportunities.

Mentors become trusted advisers and role models. They support and encourage by offering suggestions and knowledge, both general and specific. The goal is to help mentees improve their skills and, hopefully, advance their careers. As stated by Canning (2009):

> *For a leader the ultimate trust is 'letting go' of staff, empowering them to grow as practitioners and to support them in gaining ownership of their roles and responsibilities.*

Clearly, this 'letting go' needs a lot of preparation and mentoring is a good way of ensuring that preparation is in place.

Mentoring can be rewarding for you, both personally and professionally. Through it, not only can you build a stronger and more successful team, but you can also improve your leadership and communication skills, learn new perspectives and ways of thinking, and gain a strong sense of personal satisfaction. Mentoring allows you to strengthen your coaching and leadership skills by working with individuals from different backgrounds and with different personality types. Your ability to manage people different from you is a valuable skill, especially as the workplace continues to grow more diverse. Besides enhancing your skills, mentoring can improve your performance (Whalley, 2008). One of your roles as a mentor is to set a good example for your mentee. Knowing that you are responsible for providing appropriate and accurate guidance to him or her motivates you to work harder. Furthermore, mentoring can give you a fresh perspective on your performance; mentoring experience gives new insights into your own job. Mentees always ask 'Why?' – 'Why do we do things a certain way and why do I think and act the way I do?' The questions will help you to take a critical look at how you are leading and what areas you need to adjust for improvement.

Your role as a mentor can contribute to the success of your entire organisation. As an Early Years manager, you know the importance of developing and retaining good employees. By priming promising employees to become top-performing team members and by providing them with the challenges, support and commitment needed to keep them in your organisation, your mentoring efforts effectively address issues of succession planning and retention. Rather than always advertising outside the organisation for new management staff, through a mentorship scheme you will be able to consider developing talent within the organisation and have the confidence to promote from within.

By becoming a mentor, you create a legacy that has a lasting impact on your mentee and on your organisation. Not only will you gain the satisfaction of helping to develop future management talent, the knowledge you foster in your mentee can inspire new ideas for generations to come. Furthermore, through mentoring, you can help carry on your organisation's legacy by passing on its values and mission to your mentee.

For potential mentees, the benefits of mentoring can be huge. While the primary intent of your mentoring role is to challenge the mentee to think in new and different ways, they also get focused coaching and training from a skilled, knowledgeable and experienced individual, and assistance and advice in navigating the many tricky situations that can arise in the workplace. This can help them work more effectively, overcome obstacles and, therefore, improve the quality of their work. Having a mentor can have many benefits, such as:

- improving your self-confidence;
- helping you decide what to do about a particular problem;
- giving you information you might not know how to get from anywhere else;
- helping you get things off your chest and making you feel supported;
- having someone to listen, non-judgementally, to what you have to say.

In Early Years settings we often have 'leaders by accident'. In the past, leaders in early childhood settings entered into the role with little formal education or preparation. This needs to change, given that the role is so complex. Having a mentor offers great support and encouragement as Early Years practitioners progress through their careers.

Relationships may last a lifetime and are often developed with people who have been a long-term and positive influence on our development. A mentor is someone who has the unusual and valuable qualities that mean, whatever else is happening, they maintain a genuine interest in your continued development.

CHAPTER SUMMARY

- This chapter has encouraged you to think about the challenges that will face Early Years practitioners in the coming years.
- It has stressed the importance of your CPD for the sake of the whole sector.
- It has offered a rationale for you to consider taking up a mentoring role with your staff to encourage them to become the leaders of the future.

REFERENCES

Canning, N (2009) *Empowering Communities Through Inspirational Leadership*, in Robins, A and Callan, S (Editor) *Managing Early Years Settings*. London: Sage.

Chandiramani, R (2010) *Children and Young People Now*. www.cypnow.co.uk/news (accessed 15 May 2010).

CWDC (2008) *Guidance to the Standards for the Award of Early Years Professional Status*. Leeds: CWDC.

DCSF (2007) *Children's Plan – Building Brighter Futures*. Norwich: Stationery Office.

McKimm, J and Phillips, K (2009) (Editors) *Leadership and Management in Integrated Services*. Exeter: Learning Matters.

Pound, L (2008) Leadership in the Early Years, in Miller, L and Cable, C *Professionalism in the Early Years*. London: Hodder Education.

Stationery Office (1998) *Modern Public Services for Britain*. London: Stationery Office.

Thornton, L and Brunton, P (2000) www.teachingexpertise.com/bulletins (accessed 1 March 2010).

www.**early**childhood**australia**.org.au/codeofconduct (accessed 12 February 2010).

www.cwdcouncil.org.uk/eyps

FURTHER READING

Other links that may be of interest to you, or even to refresh your memory:
www.cwdcouncil.org.uk/projects/integratedqualificationsframework.htm
www.everychildmatters.gov.uk
www.everychildmatters.gov.uk/deliveringservices/workforcereform/
www.everychildmatters.gov.uk/deliveringservices/workforcereform/childrensworkforcestrategy
www.everychildmatters.gov.uk/resources-and-practice/IG00040/

DfES (2003) *Birth to Three Matters*. London: Sure Start.

Edwards, C, Gandini, L and Forman, G (1993) T*he Hundred Languages of Children: The Reggio Emilia Approach – Advanced Reflections*. New Jersey: Ablex.

Te Whariki. The New Zealand early childhood curriculum, 1996, developed under contract to the New Zealand Ministry of Education. Downloadable from: www.tki.org.nz/r/governance/tewhariki

Index

REPEY (Researching Effective Pedagogy in the
    Early Years) project 27
reports, writing 30–2
resources for supporting learning 69–73
Rose Report 95–7
Rousseau, Jean Jacques 17
Rumbold Report 18

S
safeguarding children 58–60, 105, 118
Safeguarding Policies 59
safety fears 75
salaries, Early Years staff 114
SATs 79
schemas 78
Schön, Donald 26, 48
school meals 14, 18
school readiness 94–5
school starting ages 88–9, 92, 97–8
schools 13–14
    sponsor-managed 119
self-awareness 67
SEN *see* special educational needs
Siraj-Blatchford, Iram 57
social cues 67
social development 80–2
societal expectations 81
society, and child behaviour 67–8
Socrates 68
special educational needs (SEN) 82, 99–100
staff issues
    gender 103–6
    safe recruitment 59–60
    salaries 114
Standard Assessment Tests (SATs) 79
statutory school ages 88–9, 92, 97–8
Steiner Waldorf approach 57
study/work balance 37–8
Suggate, Sebastian 92

Sure Start Children's Centres 7, 15, 52, 56,
    116–17, 119
sustained shared thinking 27
synapses, brain 66, 75

T
Te Whariki, New Zealand 91–3
team working 51–2
    with other professionals 52–4
    with parents 54–7
    safeguarding children 58–60
Ten Year Childcare Strategy 12, 20
theorists 25
thinking, sustained shared 27
Thornton, Linda 112
training courses 112
trust, lack of 67
2020 Children and Young People's Workforce
    Strategy 17

U
unique child principle 61, 65–6, 87, 94
United Nations Convention on the Rights of
    the Child 19, 101–2

V
violent crime by children 67–8
Vygotsky, Lev 80

W
'what', 'so what', 'now what' model of
    reflection 28–9
work-based learning (WBL) 39–40
    definitions 4–5
work/study balance 37–8
writing reports 30–2

Z
zone of proximal development 80

183303

**7 DAY
BOOK**